JONAH
Fact or Fiction?

by
M. R. DE HAAN, M.D.

ZONDERVAN PUBLISHING HOUSE
GRAND RAPIDS, MICHIGAN

DEDICATION

*To many thousands who by their pray-
ers, letters and expressions of interest have
made possible the broadcasting of the messages in this book over the air,*

THIS VOLUME IS GRATEFULLY DEDICATED.

THE AUTHOR

PREFACE

The messages in this book were originally prepared for broadcasting over the combined networks of the Mutual Broadcasting System and the A.B.C. Network. They are reproduced in this volume with a minimum of editing and are presented almost word for word as they were originally broadcast. As a result there are a number of repetitions. This was intentional, and the repetitions have not been deleted, because of the importance of the subject matter.

The central theme of Jonah is the Gospel of the Death and Resurrection of Christ, and this theme is reiterated frequently because it is so generally overlooked and misunderstood. While the Book of Jonah has a diversity of applications to the sinner, the backslider, and the nation of Israel, it has only one primary interpretation. This is the message of the Gospel of the Death and Resurrection. Jesus Himself establishes this fact beyond doubt (Matt. 12: 40).

With a prayer that the messages in printed form may be blessed even more than when given over the air, this volume is sent forth to the glory of our great God and Saviour, the blessing of God's people, and the salvation of sinners.

INTRODUCTION

NO book of the Bible has been subjected to more scorn and ridicule by skeptics and infidels than the little Book of Jonah. Yet no book of the Old Testament is better authenticated, and its historical character placed beyond all shadow of doubt. The Lord Jesus Himself vouches for the historicity and literalness of Jonah by seizing upon it as a type of His own literal Death and Resurrection. In Matthew 12:40, Jesus, in answering His critics, who questioned His authority, says:

> For as Jonas was three days and three nights in the whale's belly; so shall the Son of man be three days and three nights in the heart of the earth.

This passage (also referred to in Luke 11:29, 30) immediately lifts the Book of Jonah above the realm of fiction or parable. Jesus places His stamp of approval upon the historicity of the account of the Book of Jonah. But in spite of these unmistakable words of our Lord, men have continued to discredit the record and make of it a mere allegory or fable. The attack upon Jonah proceeds from three directions:

(1) The first attack is by the infidel who rejects the entire story as being a myth and a fable. We are not to be surprised at this, for to the unregenerate mind, not only Jonah, but the entire Bible is a closed book.

> Except a man be born again, he cannot SEE . . . (John 3:3).

(2) The second attack upon the Book of Jonah is by those who accept the "inspiration" of the book, but deny its literalness. They consider it a parable or allegory with great spiritual lessons, but not a record of actual fact. All such we would remind that Jesus calls Jonah a "prophet" (Luke 11: 29). If Jonah's experience was not literal, then we can also allegorize the Death and Resurrection of Jesus, to which our Lord compares the experience of Jonah.

(3) The third method of destroying the message of Jonah is far more subtle. Sincere, earnest and godly men, who would shrink from denying the "literal" experience of Jonah in the fish, nevertheless have been used to take Jonah out of the realm of the miraculous, and reduce the account to the level of a "natural" possibility. These sincere and earnest "defenders" of the faith claim that it is entirely possible to explain Jonah's sojourn in the fish on purely natural grounds. They compass land and sea about for some form of a sea monster, which could swallow a man whole, without crushing him to death, and then have a sufficient supply of oxygen in its stomach to sustain the victim's life for three days and nights. It is therefore claimed that such a creature exists, or did exist, and reports are quoted of a sailor who was swallowed by such a monster, and after several hours was rescued alive — terribly macerated and mauled, but still alive. And then it is blazoned abroad that we have evidence and proof that the Book of Jonah is true, and the experience of the prophet possible.

But all this proves nothing. No creature has ever been found capable of doing the things credited to the fish in Jonah. Jonah, when he came out of the fish, was not mauled and macerated and half dead, but apparently well and healthy, and ready to preach. This attempt to produce "proof" that the Bible account is true is a subtle form of unbelief. God expects us to believe Him without any other evidence than His Word. We must receive it by faith. Faith is the evidence and the substance (Heb. 11:1).

This demand for "proof" of the Scripture may be sincere and motivated by the highest purposes, but remove the element of faith, and seek for evidence instead, and we destroy the message. And right here we remind the reader that the answer of Jesus in Matthew 12:40 was in response to the unbelieving Pharisees who asked for "proof" of Jesus' authority. They said:

Master, we would see a sign from thee (Matt. 12:38).

These men would not believe Jesus' word, but demanded a sign as an evidence of His authority. They wanted proof, and His answer is clear:

> An evil and adulterous generation seeketh after a sign; and there shall no sign be given to it, but the sign of the prophet Jonas (Matt. 12:39).

But search for a fish in which a man could remain alive for three days and three nights is entirely beside the point, for Jonah was NOT ALIVE for that length of time in the belly of the fish. Jonah was DEAD for three days and three nights, and then was resurrected and sent forth to preach. This is the miracle in Jonah, as a perfect picture of the Gospel of the Death and Resurrection of Christ. And so all the discussion about the story of Jonah, and the attempts to prove the narrative only obscure the central message of the book — the Gospel of the Death and Resurrection of Jesus.

Tradition has so obscured the real message of Jonah, that we felt that a series of messages, divorced from traditional beliefs would be both timely and profitable. May we ask the reader to withhold criticism and reserve judgment of the views expressed until the complete volume has been read, and compared with the record in the Word of God. Whether you then agree or not, will be unimportant, if it has driven you to the Book to study anew and afresh this important and little-understood book of the prophet Jonah.

M. R. DE HAAN

Grand Rapids, Michigan

CONTENTS

Chapter One

JONAH – FACT OR FICTION?

THE Book of Jonah is the story of a man, a prophet of the Lord, who had one of the strangest experiences in all of human history. The place from which he prophesied was the bottom of the sea. The pulpit from which he preached was the stomach of a fish. Yet striking as are the circumstances of his prophecy, still more striking was the prophecy itself, for Jonah preached the Gospel of the Death and the Resurrection of the Lord Jesus Christ, eight hundred years before Christ was born. The entire Old Testament contains no clearer type, no more definite picture of the Death and Resurrection of our Saviour than the Book of Jonah. According to our Lord's own words, Jonah's experience in the belly of the fish was a picture of Himself in the tomb. Here are our Lord's words in Matthew 12:

> For as Jonas was three days and three nights in the whale's belly; so shall the Son of man be three days and three nights in the heart of the earth (Matt. 12:40).

These words were spoken in answer to the demand of the unbelieving scribes and Pharisees for a sign from heaven to authenticate the ministry of Christ. They refused to believe His WORD, and demanded a sign, and Jesus answered:

> An evil and adulterous generation seeketh after a sign; and there shall no sign be given to it, but the sign of the prophet Jonas (Matt. 12:39).

And then follow the words of our Lord Jesus Christ:

> For as Jonas was three days and three nights in the whale's belly; so shall the Son of man be three days and three nights in the heart of the earth (Matt. 12:40).

BELIEVE THE GOSPEL

These words of our Lord are inexhaustibly rich in revelation. Notice first of all, that Jesus here authenticates the historicity of the Book of Jonah. He calls Jonah a "prophet" and refers to him as a real character in history. Just why did Jesus single out the Book of Jonah to illustrate His Death and Resurrection, and to authenticate His ministry? There are many, many other pictures of death and resurrection in the Old Testament which Christ might have used, but instead He chose only Jonah.

We have, for instance, a clear shadow of the Gospel of the Death and Resurrection of Christ in the very beginning of the Bible. In Genesis Chapter 1 we have the earth rising out of the waters of judgment and life appearing upon the earth. It was the third day of creation that the dry land emerged from the waters of death, and brought forth life, for on this third day the vegetation was created. The first mention, therefore, of life upon the earth was in this account. It is a picture of death and resurrection.

Or take, for instance, the ark of Noah resting on the seventeenth day of the seventh month on Mount Ararat after being engulfed in the flood of death. Why did the Holy Spirit register the exact date, the seventeenth day of the seventh month, when the ark was free from the flood waters (Gen. 8:4)? The answer is clear when we remember that the Passover Feast came on the fourteenth day of this same month. The Passover is a picture of the death of Christ. And then He arose three days later, on the seventeenth day of the month. Here then is an indisputable picture of death and resurrection way back in the Book of Genesis.

Or take, if you will, the case of the sacrifice of Isaac on Mount Moriah. Abraham had bound Isaac on the altar, and to all intents and purposes, Isaac was dead. For three days Isaac was potentially dead in the mind of Abraham, but after these three days of agony, he was restored to him again on Mount Moriah. Abraham certainly expected Isaac to arise again, for in Hebrews 11 we read that Abraham accounted:

> . . . that God was able to raise him up, even from the dead; from whence also he received him in a figure (Heb. 11:19).

This was the Gospel of Death and Resurrection.

Or, let us take the case of Joseph. He too was in the place of death, but was exalted to the throne of Egypt, a picture of death and resurrection. Or the passage of Israel through the Red Sea might be taken as another example. Paul tells us in I Corinthians 10 that this was a figure of baptism, and baptism is a picture of the Burial and Resurrection of Christ. And so we might go on and on, and find illustrations and types of the Death and Resurrection of Christ throughout the Old Testament. It was undoubtedly to these incidents that Paul referred when he said in I Corinthians 15:

> . . . that Christ died for our sins according to the Scriptures; And that he was buried, and that he rose again the third day ACCORDING TO THE SCRIPTURES (I Cor. 15:3, 4).

The only Scriptures Paul could have referred to were the Old Testament books, and in these, the apostle says, the Death and Resurrection of Christ are clearly predicted and foreshadowed.

In view of the fact, therefore, that the Old Testament abounds with so many clear types of the Death and Resurrection of Christ, it becomes a matter of tremendous significance, that our Lord, when He wanted to select from all these Old Testament types just one which pointed to Him, He made the deliberate choice of just this one, the experience of the prophet Jonah in the belly of the fish, choosing this incident and this one alone. By picking Jonah from among all the other available types of death and resurrection with which the Old Testament abounds, He raised the Book of Jonah out of the realm of doubt and speculation, above all question of fiction or parable, and established the book as infallibly inspired, and the events in the book as an actual, literal account of a historic experience and event.

CHRIST ANSWERS THE CRITICS

The Lord knew that the Book of Jonah would be more persistently attacked and denied by the enemies of the Bible than probably any other portion of Scripture, except the first three chapters of Genesis. No other portion of the Bible has suffered so much at the hands of both enemies and friends. Well does the enemy know that to reject the Book of Jonah is to reject the Gospel of the Death and Resurrection of Jesus Christ. In no other book do we have as clear a prophecy of this Gospel of the Death and Resurrection of Christ as in the Book of Jonah. Since the Devil hates the Gospel, and Jonah is the clearest picture of the Gospel in prophecy, it is, therefore, no wonder that he has so desperately attacked this book.

SKEPTICS RIDICULE JONAH

As a result, skeptics and infidels have made sport of Jonah, and denied its literalness. Jonah, they tell us, is a figment of the imagination, a fairy tale, a parable, and has no basis in fact. The seriousness of this position is not sufficiently understood by the average believer. To deny Jonah's experience is to deny the Gospel of the Lord Jesus Christ, for He Himself said: "For as Jonah . . . so shall the Son of man be." As Jonah—so Christ. If the story of Jonah, therefore, is fiction, then so is the Gospel. If the story of Jonah is not true, then neither are the gospel records of Matthew, Mark, Luke and John reliable and true.

Faith in the Book of Jonah, therefore, is an acid test of

orthodoxy. If you want to know if a man is orthodox and sound in the Scriptures, ask him his opinion of the Book of Jonah. If he denies the story of Jonah, he will deny the Gospel. There are those who tell us that the Book of Jonah was written after the exile and captivity of Israel, and, therefore, does not record an actual literal account. The Holy Spirit also foreknew this attack upon the historicity of Jonah, and so inserted a foolproof account of the actual literal existence of this prophet. This record is tucked away in that seldom read book of II Kings. The writer of II Kings records in chapter 14 the story of Jeroboam who reigned over Israel some 800 years B.C. He restored some of the territory of Israel previously lost to the enemy. The record reads as follows:

> He restored the coast of Israel from the entering of Hamath unto the sea of the plain, according to the word of the Lord God of Israel, which he spake by the hand of his servant Jonah, the son of Amittai, the prophet, which was of Gath-hepher (II Kings 14:25).

Here then we are definitely told that Jonah was a literal prophet, who had prophesied of the events which happened as recorded in this chapter. Now we have spent all this time in these introductory statements on the Book of Jonah to show the utter inconsistency of those who would destroy the Book of Jonah, and thereby destroy the Gospel of the Lord Jesus Christ.

But there is another far more subtle way of destroying the message of Jonah than a flat denial of its genuineness. It is the effort on the part of well-meaning but misguided fundamentalists to explain the miracles in Jonah on a naturalistic basis. They seek to prove that a man could actually live in the belly of a fish for many hours and still come out alive. They think they are doing a great service to the Lord by proving on a natural plane the possibility of Jonah's sojourn in the whale without dying, but in so doing, they emasculate and destroy the whole purpose of the record. The experience of Jonah was a miracle, a supernatural miracle, which was naturally impossible, and could not be explained upon any natural basis. If it could be proven that there is a fish that could swallow a man without mutilating him, and for three days keep him in his stomach without digesting him, there would be nothing miraculous in the story of Jonah. But in so doing, we would also rob the Resurrection of Christ of its miraculous, supernatural character, for Jesus said, we remind you again:

> As Jonas was three days and three nights in the whale's belly; so shall the Son of man be three days and three nights in the heart of the earth (Matt. 12:40).

M<small>UST</small> B<small>E</small> <small>A</small> M<small>IRACLE</small>

This attempt, therefore, to explain Jonah by natural reasoning and scientific investigation is a trick of the enemy to destroy the supernatural character of the Gospel which the story of Jonah illustrates. One of the most subtle attacks upon the Word of God is the attempt to PROVE the Bible. Men compass land and sea about, dig into the ruins of ancient Bible cities, and then expect us to become excited when they come up with some archaeological discovery which finally PROVES the Bible to be true. What a clever scheme of the enemy to cause us to seek PROOF outside of the Scripture itself. The true believer in the Lord Jesus Christ needs no external proof of the authenticity of the Word of God. He has the witness within himself, for he has had an experience of its truthfulness. He believes it because God says it.

The Bible does not need the endorsement of science. It does not need the proof of archaeology. The Bible needs no apologies and no defense. It has stood on its own record and merit for millenniums while the so-called scientific objections have fallen and mouldered in the dust of antiquity. Before there was any archaeology the Bible was able to stand on its own feet. The older I become the more I see the folly of trying to prove the Bible. Our ministry is not apologetic, but the positive preaching of "Thus saith the Lord." The late Dr. William L. Pettingill used to say, "Talk about defending the Bible? Why, you might as well talk about defending a lion. Let him loose. He'll defend himself."

All of this, therefore, is implied in the very first verse of the Book of Jonah. In Jonah 1:1 we read:

Now the word of the Lord came unto Jonah.

The Book of Jonah, therefore, opens with a reminder that we are dealing with the WORD OF THE LORD, and not the word of man. It is not the word of man, but God's own testimony, and surely God does not have to explain His reason for doing things to His puny, insignificant creatures. What brazen presumption to question what God says. As though the Creator must stoop to the credulity of His creature, man would call God into an account why He does what He does.

SHOW US A SIGN

Which brings us back just where we started in Matthew 12. There the scribes and Pharisees refused to believe Jesus' WORDS, but demanded tangible evidence and a sign from heaven. They said. "Show us a sign from heaven." Perform a miracle and we'll believe You, and Jesus' only answer to them is the answer which has come down through the centuries:

An evil and adulterous generation seeketh after a sign; and there shall no sign be given to it, but the sign of the prophet Jonas (Matt. 12:39).

This, beloved, is still as true today as when the Lord Jesus spoke those words. God will not condescend to prove His Word, or give any more evidence than we have in this Book itself. We are to believe it, and to be saved. We are not expected to understand all of it. We are not to look for feelings or for signs or manifestations or demonstrations, but to believe it upon the simple record that God who has given it, cannot lie. And so it all depends upon our faith. Reject the Word of God, and a man is lost forever. Are you, my friend, looking for signs or wonders or miracles or some feeling before you are willing to believe the record of the Word of God? You will never get it, for God says BELIEVE. "Believe on the Lord Jesus Christ, and thou shalt be saved." He said to the scribes and Pharisees:

> There shall no sign be given . . . but the sign of the prophet Jonas (Matt. 12:39b).

This is the sign of the Gospel, and we are to believe the Gospel which records that when we were lost and undone, God sent His Only-Begotten Son into the world and gave Him for our sins, and by His Death and Resurrection, He has made possible justification for all who will believe.

> He that heareth my word, and believeth on him that sent me, hath everlasting life, and shall not come into condemnation; but is passed from death unto life (John 5:24).

Chapter Two

THE BACKSLIDDEN PREACHER

> Now the word of the Lord came unto Jonah the son of Amittai, saying,
>
> Arise, go to Nineveh, that great city, and cry against it; for their wickedness is come up before me (Jonah 1:1, 2).

THUS opens the most unusual, intriguing fish story in the entire world. Men usually listen to fish stories with suspicion and incredulity, for fish have an amazing habit of growing incredibly in both length and size after being caught, and increase with each time the story is retold. But the record of Jonah's fish story is different, because it is true. It is not exaggerated because it is recorded by the Holy Spirit Himself who inspired Jonah to put on record this amazing account.

MATTHEW TWELVE

The Lord Jesus Himself, eight hundred years later, vouches for the truthfulness of this record breaking fish story of the strangest fisherman in history, who instead of catching the fish, was caught by the fish. In Matthew 12, when His doubters asked Him for a sign to prove His authority and His divine commission, Jesus said:

> No sign shall be given to it, but the sign of the prophet Jonas:
>
> For as Jonas was three days and three nights in the whale's belly; so shall the Son of man be three days and three nights in the heart of the earth (Matt. 12:39b, 40).

In these brief, simple words (also recorded in Luke 11), Jesus, therefore, lifts the blanket of doubt and suspicion from

17

the Book of Jonah, and puts His stamp of authenticity upon
the entire narrative. Either the story of Jonah is true, or it
is false. Jesus said, however, that it is true, and so He either
spoke the truth or Jesus becomes a liar. From this evidence
it is clear that to doubt the story of Jonah is to doubt the
Gospel of the Lord Jesus Christ. It is, therefore, of tremendous importance to believe the story of Jonah and the
fish. Just as important as to believe John 3:16. To deny the
historicity of the sojourn of Jonah in the belly of the whale
for three days and three nights is to deny the historicity
of the Lord Jesus Christ and His Death and Resurrection. For
let us repeat, the Lord says, "As Jonah was . . . so shall the
Son of man be." If Jonah was NOT, then the Son of Man was
NOT. Jesus taught that Jonah was a historical character. If
then the skeptic is right and the Book of Jonah is but a mere
allegory, a myth, or a parable, then Jesus was either tragically
ignorant and deceived or maliciously dishonest. Our Lord
Himself calls Jonah a "prophet," who was three days and
three nights in the belly of the fish, and compares his experience with His own death, in the three days' entombment
and His Resurrection from the dead. As Jonah . . . so also
the Son of man. There is no mistaking these words. As
Jonah . . . so also Christ.

A BOOK OF MIRACLES

We need not wonder at the miraculous element in the
story of the fish. The Book of Jonah abounds in miracles.
It was a miracle that Jonah was preserved for three days
and three nights in the belly of the fish, but it was also a
miracle of grace that Nineveh was spared. It was a miracle
that a gourd could spring up overnight and overshadow Jonah.
It was a miracle that a little worm could destroy the vine in
just a few moments. The book, therefore, is full of miracles,
and yet the one miracle against which all the attacks of the
enemy are directed is the miracle of Jonah in the belly of the

fish. We hear little objection to the miracle of the supernatural gourd, or the worm, or the stilling of the storm, but
the one incident in the Book of Jonah upon which almost all
attacks are leveled is the story of his sojourn in the belly of
the fish. The reason for this becomes immediately evident.
Jonah's death in the fish and his resurrection are a picture of
the Gospel of the Death and Resurrection of Christ. That is
why the enemies of the Gospel can swallow the storm, they
can swallow the vine, and even are willing to swallow the
worm, but the fish — the fish — that just it too big a mouth-
ful for them. Jesus leaves no doubt in the matter, but has
linked His own Death and Resurrection upon which our
salvation absolutely depends, directly with the deliverance
of Jonah from the belly of the great fish.

THE OPENING VERSE

We call your attention again to the opening verse of Jonah
which tells of the authority of this book. It reads:

> Now the word of the Lord came unto Jonah the son of
> Amittai, saying . . . (Jonah 1:1).

Jonah, the prophet had a divine commission, and it is
stated here that it was the actual "word of the Lord." Just
how the word of the Lord came to Jonah we are not told.
Whether Jonah heard an audible voice, whether the Lord
appeared to Him in human form, as a theophany, we are not
told. It might have been by vision, or a dream. After all, it
does not matter. He had his divine orders and he was expected to obey them.

Before taking up Jonah's commission, just a word about
the man himself. Jonah, as we know, was a type of the Lord
Jesus in his Death and Resurrection. As such his name is
significant. The name Jonah means a "Dove." Now the dove
is a symbol of peace, mildness, and harmlessness. Doves are
meek, mournful and harmless as described in Scripture. The
first mention of a dove is found in Genesis 8:8. Here the

dove was released from the ark by Noah, and it returned with an olive branch in its beak, bringing the good news of deliverance from the flood of waters. The dove, therefore, becomes the bringer of good news. The good news is the Gospel of the Death and the Resurrection of Christ of which the flood was a typical picture.

Jonah, therefore, as a type of Christ in his sojourn in the belly of the fish, proclaimed the good news of the Gospel of salvation. But a dove also had another significance. In the offerings of Israel God made provision for the sacrifice of bulls and heifers, goats and calves and sheep for those who could afford them. But if the offerer were too poor to bring one of these animals, then the Lord allowed him to bring an offering of doves, the commonest and the cheapest of birds, especially for the use of the poorer people of Israel (Lev. 5:7). It all speaks of the one of whom Jonah was a type. The Lord Jesus was the personification of meekness and mourning. He came to preach deliverance to the captives and the Gospel to the poor. He was born in poverty, for when His mother Mary brought her sacrifice for Him (Luke 2:23, 24) she brought the poor man's offering, and we read:

> And when the days of her purification according to the law of Moses were accomplished, they brought him to Jerusalem, to present him to the Lord;
> And to offer a sacrifice according to that which is said in the law of the Lord, A pair of turtledoves, or two young pigeons (Luke 2:22, 24).

The very name Jonah, the "dove," therefore, gives us the key to the book, for it is the picture of the lowly Jesus who for our sakes became poor, that we through His poverty might be rich. But further, will you notice that the name of his father is Amittai, and means "truth." Jonah was the son of truth. And He of whom Jonah prophesied was Himself the "truth," for He said:

> I am the way, the truth, and the life: no man cometh unto the Father, but by me (John 14:6).

The first word which the Lord spoke to Jonah also gives us a glimpse as to the characteristics of this temperamental and sentimental man. In Jonah 1:2 we read:

> Arise, go to Nineveh, that great city, and cry against it; for their wickedness is come up before me.

This verse gives us a glimpse of Jonah, the man. We are amazed that a man so frail, so temperamental, so lazy, so disobedient could be used as a type of the perfect Son of God. But all this only exalts the grace of God. It is so with all the types. We think of David, for instance, the backslider, the adulterer, the murderer, and yet he is used as a type of the Lord Jesus. It is a miracle of God's grace that He can use fallible, stumbling men to exalt His grace and bring His message. So it was in the case of Jonah. What a mess Jonah presents to us. Fickle-minded, unstable, cowardly, backslidden, temperamental Jonah, yet God was willing to use him. Oh, the matchless grace of God.

ARISE

God's first word to Jonah was "arise." Evidently Jonah was sitting or lying down at the time. He was enjoying himself and was at ease while the world was rushing to its doom. "Arise, Jonah, get up lazybones, there is work to be done," God seems to say. Jonah was evidently an easy-going, lackadaisical sort of a person. He not only was lying or sitting down when God called him, but later we find him fast asleep in the midst of a great storm. How sad that even believers can fall asleep in the midst of the storm. It reminds us of another passage in the Scriptures in Romans where Paul admonishes us:

> It is high time to awake out of sleep: for now is our salvation nearer than when we believed.
> The night is far spent, the day is at hand: let us therefore cast off the works of darkness, and let us put on the armour of light (Rom. 13:11, 12).

Or listen to Paul in Ephesians:

> Awake thou that sleepest, and arise from the dead, and Christ shall give thee light.
>
> See then that ye walk circumspectly, not as fools, but as wise,
>
> Redeeming the time, because the days are evil (Eph. 5:14-16).

OUR COMMISSION

The word of the Lord to Jonah "arise and go" is the word of the Lord to every believer in this dispensation. For Nineveh certainly represents a lost world, tottering on the brink of doom and destruction, and heading for everlasting punishment. And yet with millions and millions dying today without Christ, the Church of the Lord Jesus has been lolling in ease and luxury. In these days of boom and prosperity we have somehow like Jonah settled down to enjoy our salvation, and have closed our eyes and ears to the plight of the millions about us without the Lord Jesus Christ. How long since you, my Christian brother, have talked to some soul for the Lord Jesus Christ? What proportion of your time and talent do you give to let others know the story of redeeming grace? We would cry out to you, as the shipmaster did to Jonah in verse six:

> What meanest thou, O sleeper? arise, call upon thy God, if so be that God will think upon us, that we perish not (Jonah 1:6).

THE MESSAGE

Before we come to the end of this chapter on Jonah, will you notice the message which the Lord had committed to him. It was a message of judgment.

> . . . go to Nineveh . . . and cry against it, for their wickedness is come up before me (Jonah 1:2).

It was not a wish-washy message of telling sinners that God was a God of love and He will not punish the wicked. Ah, no, it was a weighty message of dire judgment. Later on in the book we read in greater detail the message which Jonah delivered:

Yet forty days, and Nineveh shall be overthrown (Jonah 3:4b).

This was the message which God had given to Jonah. The Lord had borne with their wickedness a long, long time in tenderness and in compassion, and now He sets a deadline. Forty days, and unless Nineveh repents the judgment of God must fall. The number "forty" in Scripture is the number of probation, the number of the limit of testing. Forty years Israel was tested in the wilderness. Forty days Israel was tested while Moses was in the mountain. Forty days Jesus was tested and proven in the wilderness.

Then at the end of the probation period comes the deadline. This was the message of Jonah. God will not always chide with men, and His patience will not go on forever. There comes a time when judgment must fall unless the warning of the Word of God and God's servants is heeded. And so we would like to make this lesson direct and practical and personal to both saint and sinner. Child of God do you realize that the day of opportunity is not going to last forever? The time for serving Christ, telling the story of redemption, bringing forth fruit is limited. God has set a deadline for you, when the day of your opportunity will come to an end. Today may be that day! Before another day dawns you may be one of the thousands in this world who will never see tomorrow. Today may be the end of the "forty days" for you. And then, you will stand before the Judge of heaven and earth to give an account of what you have done for Him.

Therefore let us not sleep, as do others; but let us watch and be sober.

For they that sleep, sleep in the night; and they that be drunken are drunken in the night.

But let us, who are of the day, be sober, putting on the breastplate of faith and love; and for an helmet, the hope of salvation.

> For God hath not appointed us to wrath, but to obtain sal-
> vation by our Lord Jesus Christ (I Thess. 5:6-9).

But sinner, for you the case is still worse. There comes a day when God will call you to faith and repentance for the very last time. One of these days as surely as you were born your life will also come to an end. One of these days you will listen to the last sermon and the last invitation, and this day may be it. Yes, this may be it! This may be the last day of your forty days of probation which God is willing to give you. And then — the judgment. God's deadline is fixed unalterably.

> . . . it is appointed unto men once to die, and after this the
> judgment (Heb. 9:27).

God will not promise to save anyone tomorrow. Tomorrow may be too late. For "now is the accepted time," today if ye will hear His voice, harden not your heart. Oh, will you honestly ask yourself the question, "Is today God's deadline for me?"

"Believe on the Lord Jesus Christ, and thou shalt be saved."

Chapter Three

THE SLEEPING PROPHET

> But Jonah rose up to flee unto Tarshish from the presence of the Lord, and went down to Joppa; and he found a ship going to Tarshish: so he paid the fare thereof, and went down into it, to go with them unto Tarshish from the presence of the Lord (Jonah 1:3).

"BUT Jonah rose up to flee . . . from the presence of the Lord." God had commanded Jonah to arise and go to Nineveh and preach the coming judgment upon that city. But—but—Jonah did exactly the opposite. He arose all right, not to obey the Lord, but to follow his own desires and inclinations. Instead of going east, he started directly west, and here is a picture of Jonah, the backslider.

The Book of Jonah has many, many applications. We know, of course, that Jonah was primarily and first of all the type of the Death and Resurrection of the Lord Jesus Christ. We must never lose sight of this. But Jonah is also a type of the sinner for whom Christ came to die. And so, before seeing Jonah in the belly of the fish as a type of the substitutionary work of Christ, we want to see the sad plight of those for whom He died. The story is replete with lessons.

FOOLISH BACKSLIDER

Notice first of all, how sin blinds the eyes of God's servant, and twists his reasoning. Jonah was a servant of the Lord, a prophet called of God with a divine message. Jonah knew the Lord, and knew that the Lord had called him. And so it is hard to understand how he could be so foolish as to imagine that he could run away from the Lord. Our text states that Jonah "rose up to flee . . . from the presence of the Lord." Now Jonah knew better than that, but his disobedience twisted his judgment, blinded his eyes into imagining that he could get away with it. Jonah must have been familiar with the words of David in Psalm 139 written many years before:

> Whither shall I go from thy spirit? or whither shall I flee from thy presence?
> If I ascend up into heaven, thou art there: if I make my bed in hell, behold, thou art there.
> If I take the wings of the morning, and dwell in the uttermost parts of the sea;
> Even there shall thy hand lead me, and thy right hand shall hold me.
> If I say, Surely the darkness shall cover me; even the night shall be light about me.
> Yea, the darkness hideth not from thee; but the night shineth as the day: the darkness and the light are both alike to thee (Ps. 139:7-12).

What fools God's children become when they live in disobedience to His will and Word, and blind themselves to the truth of God.

GOD FOLLOWS HIS OWN

But notice where Jonah went. We read he went "down" to Joppa. He went DOWN. The path of disobedience is always "DOWN." Jonah kept on going down until he returned to the Lord. First, he went DOWN to Joppa, then he went DOWN into the ship, then he went DOWN into the sea, then DOWN the gullet of a fish, and finally, DOWN into sheol itself. There is no standing still in the path of disobedience. You either stop and return to the Lord, or go down and down and down.

But God's eye was on Jonah all the time, even though he was trying to forget the Lord. Even though the child of God seeks to flee and hide from God in his disobedience, the Lord will not let His erring child go, and so we read in verse 4:

But the Lord (Jonah 1:4a).

We want to stop right there. "But the Lord." Notice how verse three also opens with a "But." "But Jonah rose up to flee." That was Jonah's BUT in answer to God's call. However, God has a BUT which completely rules out and negates Jonah's BUT. When God tells His children to do something there are no "ifs or buts" about it. God answered Jonah's BUT with God's BUT, and the verse follows:

But the Lord sent out a great wind into the sea, and there was a mighty tempest in the sea, so that the ship was like to be broken (Jonah 1:4).

Man proposes, but God disposes. Jonah had forgotten that the command to go was an absolute, inviolable command. God is going to have His way with us and we are going to fit into God's plan no matter what it takes. But there are two ways that this can be accomplished. One is by willing submission, and the other is by painful constraint. How much easier would it have been for Jonah to go willingly, than to make it necessary for God to force him to go through his terrible experience. However, God has a way of making us obedient. In the case of Jonah it was through a storm, a tempest and a harrowing experience inside a fish. What trouble Jonah could have spared himself if he had only immediately obeyed and said, "Lord, here am I, send me." In the end he had to go anyway, THE HARD WAY.

MANY EXCUSES

I do not know what particular excuse Jonah gave for going west instead of east, to Tarshish instead of Nineveh. But he undoubtedly had some excuse, probably many of them, even though he did not have one good reason. When we are unwilling to do God's will we can always find an excuse. When God wants us to contact some soul, make some call,

do some service for Him, how easy it is for us to excuse ourselves. We haven't the time. We are too busy, or we don't
feel well, or some other trivial excuses are offered to God.
But God says, "Arise, and go."

And notice too, that when we are looking for excuses to
disobey the Lord, the devil always makes it easy for us to find
excuses. When Jonah turned his face from God toward
Tarshish, the Devil had a ship all ready and waiting for
Jonah. He even saw to it that Jonah had the price of a ticket
for he "paid the fare thereof." Satan himself will see to it
that he makes it easy for you to go in the opposite direction
from which the Lord is calling you.

BUT GOD

But it was all of no avail for God followed Jonah every
step of the way. A mighty storm arose and the ship was like
to be broken. Jonah was not hidden from God. And now
notice the sad, sad results of Jonah's backsliding. Others who
were not partakers of his disobedience had to suffer for his
sin. Notice the plight of others in Jonah's case:

> Then the mariners were afraid, and cried every man unto
> his god, and cast forth the wares that were in the ship into
> the sea, to lighten it of them. But Jonah was gone down into
> the sides of the ship; and he lay, and was fast alseep (Jonah
> 1:5).

Jonah's disobedience brought disaster not only upon himself, but upon others as well. It is a solemn truth that no
man can sin alone and suffer for it alone. Jonah's sin was
visited upon these innocent sailors. We may rebel against this
truth, but it is a fact, that because one man sins, others must
suffer. Children suffer for the sins of the parents, citizens
suffer for the mistakes of their rulers. It is the law of life.
We are social beings, inseparably interdependent upon each
other, and even our personal acts have their social results.
No man can sin by himself. How we ought to realize this.
Here is the drunkard who says, "If I want to be a drunk and

end up in a pauper's grave it is no one's business but my own." But it is someone else's business. What he says is absolutely not true. If a man is a drunkard, he not only suffers, but his children and his neighbors whose lives he endangers suffer as well. The whole nation pays when this man is put in prison, and later becomes a state charge as an alcoholic. Thousands of examples might be cited to show that sin is never an individual thing at all, but has its social implications.

The Bible tells us that the sins of the fathers are visited upon the children to the third and fourth generations. We repeat, therefore, that there are no private sins, for our sins do affect others as well as ourselves.

AWAKE, SLEEPER

Now we come to a most tragic illustration of the result of sin and disobedience in the lives of God's people. Sin is a narcotic, a spiritual anesthetic which beclouds reason, stifles conviction, twists character and perverts our will. Notice the record in Jonah. While the storm was raging, the winds howling, the waves dashing and the ship creaking, we read:

> But Jonah was gone down into the sides of the ship; and he lay, and was fast asleep (Jonah 1:5b).

What a tragedy! What a scene! Because of his sin others were in peril of death and he lay quietly sleeping. Asleep while judgment was impending, while death threatened not only himself, but others as well. The backslider, too, is unconscious of his peril and the awfulness of his sin. For sin is a paralyzing force. When the backslider admits he has backslidden, he is not backslidden anymore. No Christain who is out of the will of the Lord will admit that he is out of God's will. He will seek to justify and excuse his condition as long as possible, but the moment he recognizes his awful condition and is willing to admit that he is a backslider, he is back on the road to restoration.

But the world knows better. The world is quick to recognize the inconsistency of the sleeping Christian, and quick to condemn the inconsistent believers. So the shipmaster came to Jonah and said unto him:

> What meanest thou, O sleeper? arise, call upon thy God, if so be that God will think upon us, that we perish not (Jonah 1:6).

What meanest thou, O sleeper? Would to God that all of us might take this rebuke to our hearts personally. We profess to believe the Word of the Living God, and have accepted Christ as our Saviour. We believe (or say we believe) that men and women are lost without Christ, and on the road to an eternal hell. We believe that the Bible teaches a literal place of eternal darkness for the rejecters of Christ and that only the Gospel can save men and women from this destruction. We believe (or at least we say we believe) the Bible which says that the lost "shall go away into everlasting punishment" (Matt. 25:46).

I wonder whether we really believe this or whether it is only an item in our creed. Listen to Paul in II Thessalonians:

> And to you who are troubled rest with us, when the Lord Jesus shall be revealed from heaven with his mighty angels,
> In flaming fire taking vengeance on them that know not God, and that obey not the gospel of our Lord Jesus Christ:
> Who shall be punished with everlasting destruction from the presence of the Lord, and from the glory of his power;
> When he shall come to be glorified in his saints, and to be admired in all them that believe (II Thess. 1:7-10).

Again I say, I wonder whether we believe these inspired words of the Scriptures. Let us listen to John in Revelation 21:8:

> But the fearful, and unbelieving, and the abominable, and murderers, and whoremongers, and sorcerers, and idolaters, and all liars, shall have their part in the lake which burneth with fire and brimstone: which is the second death (Rev. 21:8).

Again I say, I wonder whether we believe that these words are true and binding. I have neither the desire nor the strength to describe in lurid terms the agonies of the damned in hell, and so the best that I can do is to simply let the loving, gentle Jesus give you His own description of the doom which awaits sinners round about us. The word "hell" occurs eleven times in the New Testament, and in every instance (except one) it comes from the lips of the gentle, compassionate Christ. He describes it as a place where the worm never dies and where the fire is never quenched. It is called in Revelation 19, a lake of fire. It will be the everlasting abode of the Devil and his angels. For in Revelation we read:

> And the devil that deceived them was cast into the lake of fire and brimstone, where the beast and the false prophet are, and shall be tormented day and night for ever and ever (Rev. 20:10).

This language is unmistakable. We do not preach on this subject by choice, but by compulsion and by constraint. It gives us no pleasure to announce the doom of the wicked and we can understand Jonah's aversion to bringing this message of doom to Nineveh. We would to God that we did not have to believe in the awful subject of hell and eternal punishment. Like Jonah, we would like to run away from the preaching of the judgment message, but we have no choice. We preach it only because it is in the Book, and because we believe that it is real. We preach it with a broken heart, and with weeping eyes. We could wish that there were no eternal hell and if we followed our own sentiments we would dismiss the existence of such a place altogether.

But since we believe the Bible clearly teaches the eternal doom of sinners in the place prepared for the Devil and his angels in the Lake of Fire, we should be despicable brutes not to warn men and women about it. If we do NOT believe it then we are cruel sadists to scare men and women with its threatenings, but if we do believe it, how can we be silent about it.

If I knew that down the railroad a bridge was washed out, and then stood complacently by the tracks without warning the engineer while the train thundered by, what would you think of me? If I knew that you had a deadly disease but also had in my possession the remedy to cure you, but did nothing about it, what would you call me? But what about Christians who believe the Bible, who know that men are lost, who know there is an eternal hell, and fail to shout at the top of their voices to those about them?

> Flee from the wrath to come (Luke 3:7b).

The Word of the Lord came unto Jonah saying, "Arise and go — and preach unto it the preaching that I bid thee."

> Cry aloud, spare not, lift up thy voice like a trumpet, and shew my people their transgression, and the house of Jacob their sins (Isa. 58:1).

The message of Jonah then was a message of judgment. Until the sinner sees God's judgment upon sin, he will never seek God's salvation. The background of Calvary was judgment. Calvary is a picture of God's judgment upon sin. But now here comes the good news. Nineveh repented at the preaching of Jonah and was spared. And the reason that we too preach judgment, is only that we may show men the awful doom which awaits them without Christ, so that they may be prepared for the message of salvation and be saved. You can be saved from hell and judgment by believing God's Word, not only concerning your lost condition, but also the wonderful remedy which Christ Jesus has given in the Book:

> Verily, verily, I say unto you, He that heareth my word, and believeth on him that sent me, hath everlasting life, and shall not come into condemnation; but is passed from death unto life (John 5:24).

Chapter Four

SHAKING DICE IN A PINCH

And they said every one to his fellow, Come, and let us cast lots, that we may know for whose cause this evil is upon us. So they cast lots, and the lot fell upon Jonah (Jonah 1:7).

THE Bible contains many, many records of lottery. Casting lots seems to have been a well-known and common practice in situations which involved difficult decisions. In many instances it appears to be sanctioned of God and He was pleased to reveal His will by this particular method of casting the lot. But this fact that it was resorted to in certain instances with the apparent approval of God, does not in itself endorse the practice today, or give encouragement for games of chance, drawings, lotteries, betting, and the like. Only when there was no other way of ascertaining God's answer was it permitted in the Bible at all.

THE CASE OF JONAH

The casting of lots by the sailors in the book of Jonah, is a case in point. The sailors were at their wits' end and at a loss what to do. They recognized in the awful tempest something supernatural and outside the ordinary course of nature. What gave these experienced sailors this impression we do not know. It may be that they recognized in the character and the severity of the storm something which was without precedent, or it may well have been a completely unseasonable tempest. At any rate, whatever the reason may have been, they recognized that the tempest was a judgment of God for some crime or misdemeanor, and the only way they could think of identifying the guilty culprit was by resorting to the casting of lots among the sailors. Which method they used is not revealed. It may have been by the throwing of stones (dice), or by placing the names in a hat or other receptacle, or some other method, but the lot did fall upon the guilty person with his resultant confession. In this case men cast the lot, and God was pleased to give His answer according to Proverbs 16:

> The lot is cast into the lap; but the whole disposing thereof is of the Lord (Prov. 16:33).

OTHER EXAMPLES

The Old Testament abounds with examples of the use of the "lot" to ascertain the will of the Lord. In Leviticus 16:7-10, Aaron was to cast lots upon the two goats to determine which one was to be slain, and which one was to be sent away bearing the sin of Israel into the wilderness. Joshua divided the land of Canaan among the twelve tribes of Israel by lot (Josh. 18:10). In the case of Achan, the culprit who stole the spoils of Jericho, and brought defeat upon the Israelites in their attack upon the city of Ai, the guilty one was detected by the casting of lots (Josh. 7:14). Samuel evidently used the lot in determining which one of the sons of Jesse should be king, and David was indicated by this method which Samuel employed. The sons of Aaron received their cities by this casting of lots (I Chron. 6:54). The duties of the individual priests were decided by the casting of lots (I Chron. 24:5). The singers among Israel to be used in the tabernacle worship, were also chosen by lot (I Chron. 25:8-31). The porters for the house of the Lord were chosen by lot (I Chron. 26:13, Neh. 10:34).

SEEKING GOD'S WILL

From these and other passages we see that God often made known His will by the casting of lots, and men frequently resorted to this particular method of finding God's will. The method employed seems to have been by the use of stones or "dice" of different colors. One of these stones or "dice" was taken blindly from a pouch, or was cast in the lap, and the color or figures on the stone which turned up would give the answer to the problem being sought. The word for "lot" in the Old Testament is *goral*, and means a small stone or a pebble. The word in the New Testament is *die* (probably made of wood or bone). We have the word "dice" today, meaning square pieces of ivory with different numbers of spots on the six sides, and used in gambling devices. The word "dice" is the plural of *die*, and the New Testament word for lot, is *die*, and more than one would be "dice." From this we may deduce that at least one way of seeking the answer to a problem was by the use of these pebbles or dice.

Urim and Thummim

However, God sanctioned the use of casting "dice" only in the matter of seeking His divine will. It was never mentioned until Israel became a nation and seems to be limited only to the nation of Israel and the Old Testament. While revelation was still incomplete, and most of the books of the Bible were not yet written, God was pleased to reveal His will by this particular method. It was strictly forbidden for any other use or purpose. In order that Israel, therefore, with their incomplete Scriptures and their limited revelation, might come to God to find out His answer to difficult decisions which God had not made known, He gave to the high priest in the tabernacle, a set of dice for this very purpose. They are called the Urim and the Thummim, carried at all times in a pocket in the breastplate of the high priest.

Among the garments of the high priest was a breastplate. This was a square piece of cloth in five colors, white, blue, purple, scarlet and gold. This square piece of beautiful cloth hung from the shoulders over the breast of the priest. It was attached with golden rings and tied to the ephod or the coat beneath by blue ribbons or cords of lace. Set in this breastplate which hung over the breast of the high priest were twelve stones — one stone for each of the twelve tribes of Israel. This breastplate was called the breastplate of judgment or decision (Ex. 28:15).

THE POCKET IN THE BREASTPLATE

In this breastplate, or "bib," as it might be called, was a pocket or pouch serving as a receptacle for the mysterious Urim and the Thummim. In Exodus we read:

> And thou shalt put in the breastplate of judgment (decision) the Urim and the Thummim; and they shall be upon Aaron's heart, when he goeth in before the Lord (Ex. 28:30a).

While these two objects, the Urim and the Thummim are not minutely described, we may gather from their use in the experience of Israel, that they were designed to ascertain the will of the Lord in regard to Israel whenever added information was needed. In Numbers 27, Moses in commissioning Joshua commanded:

> And he (Joshua) shall stand before Eleazar the priest, who shall ask counsel for him after the judgment of the Urim before the Lord (Num. 27:21a).

Joshua then was to seek the will of God by consulting the priest, who would, through the use of the Urim and the Thummim determine the will of God for his life and the program designed for him.

It is usually agreed that the Urim and the Thummim were two stones, one white and the other one black, which the priest carried continually in the pouch of the breastplate over his heart. When the will of the Lord was to be sought, the high priest would reach into this pouch to ascertain God's answer to the particular problem by picking out one of these stones, either the Urim or the Thummim. It is thought that the white meant YES, and the black stone would mean NO! This unique method of making decisions was widely employed by the Children of Israel through the priesthood. King David while in exile and persecuted by Saul, was joined by the priest Abiathar with the ephod (I Sam. 23:6). A clear example of David's use is found in I Samuel 30:7, 8:

> And David said to Abiathar the priest, Ahimelech's son, I pray thee, bring me hither the ephod. And Abiathar brought thither the ephod to David.
>
> And David enquired at the Lord, saying, Shall I pursue after this troop? shall I overtake them? And he answered him, Pursue: for thou shalt surely overtake them, and without fail recover all.

Here we find David the King of Israel inquiring of the Lord as to the advisability of going into the battle. You will notice that the answer could be either yes, or no, and the priest undoubtedly picked out the white stone from the ephod, which meant that God favored David's going into the battle and that he would be successful.

Time prevents us from calling attention to all the other instances in the Scriptures. After the return of Judah from the Babylonian captivity, Nehemiah prevented the people from making important decisions until the priest could be found with the Urim and the Thummim in his possession (Ezra 2:63). At the destruction of Jerusalem the records and genealogies had been lost, and the people were not certain who belonged to the priesthood and so they were not to make any decision until the Urim and the Thummim could be consulted.

Is It for Us Today

But all this was under the law and applied to the nation of Israel. All this was only for this particular nation during their sojourn in the land. We, therefore, ask the question, Does this rule still apply to us today? Are we to seek the will of the Lord by casting lots? The answer, of course, is an emphatic NO! We now have the perfect expression of God"s complete will in our completed Bible. Israel had only the first few books of the Old Testament and none other. They did not have the full revelation of the will of God, and so God accommodated Himself to them, and gave them this temporary means of ascertaining His will during the time while Revelation was still incomplete.

But now that which is perfect is come, and we have no more need for additional revelation. Like signs and wonders and miracles and dreams and visions and tongues, which were for the time then present, and for the day of immaturity, the Urim and the Thummim have ceased. We now can know the will of God from the Word of God. We now have the Bible, the only rule of faith and practice for the believer, and we now have the Holy Spirit dwelling within us so that every child of God can know God's will without any other manifestation or sign. We can find the answer to every problem in the Word of God, and if we cannot find the answer, it is only because we have not yet acquainted ourselves sufficiently with God's answer book, the Bible.

GAMBLING FORBIDDEN

So in this dispensation it is wicked for Christians to ask for more than "Thus saith the Lord." Gambling is strictly forbidden by the Scriptures. Games of chance have no place in the life of the believer. Betting on the races, the numbers games, lotteries, drawing for prizes are contrary to the will and the Word of God for believers. And, of course, this goes for the other forms of seeking the unknown, such as astrology, soothsaying, witchcraft, spiritism, palmistry and fortune telling. These were not even permitted under the Old Testament economy.

WE LIVE BY FAITH

We are, therefore, to live by faith in the written Word of God, and guide our lives entirely by it. There are only two instances of casting lots in the New Testament and in both cases it was wrong. The soldiers gambled for the robe of the Lord Jesus Christ. It was a brazen and wicked act. The other instance of casting lots is in Acts chapter one. Jesus had commanded His disciples to WAIT in Jerusalem for the coming of the Holy Spirit. They were not to make a move without Him. But Peter became impatient and could not wait any longer. And so he called a congregational meeting for an election of officers in organizing the church before it was born. Now Jesus had not told him to do this, but He had told him instead to WAIT for the Holy Spirit who would direct them into all truth. But Peter suggested that they replace Judas, who had committed suicide, with another apostle. And so they set up a slate of candidates and then "shook dice" to determine the winner. Here is the record:

> And they gave forth their lots (cast the dice); and the lot fell upon Matthias; and he was numbered with the eleven apostles (Acts 1:26).

This was all a mistake, and God never recognized or accepted Matthias at all. He is never once mentioned again in the entire Scriptures. Some years later the Holy Spirit gave His choice in the apostle Paul, and he became the twelfth apostle. How we need the lesson personally in our own church life — to wait upon the Lord, and search His Word for His own will in our lives.

Our great High Priest in heaven has sent His Holy Spirit, and given us His Word as our infallible guide. On His breast He bears the breastplate with the names of all His own over His own heart. And He has the true Urim and the Thummim, and the answer to all of our problems.

Today, therefore, it is absolutely unscriptural and wicked for the Christian to resort to any gambling device or means of lottery or game of chance, but he is to walk entirely by faith. Undoubtedly in the Book of the Revelation we have a reference to this Urim and Thummim as fulfilled in the person of our great High Priest. In Revelation 2:17 we read:

> To him that overcometh . . . will I give a white stone, and in the stone a new name written.

This is the white stone of God's approval. Is your name written there?

Chapter Five

ONE MAN MUST DIE

BECAUSE one man had sinned a whole boatload of sailors was under sentence of death. Because Jonah the prophet was trying to shirk his duty, the men on board the ship on which he fled were in jeopardy of their lives. All of this becomes a picture of the world today. Because one man sinned the world lies under the judgment and the curse of his sin. Because Adam, our first father, disobeyed God, the Lord cursed all of his offspring as well as the rest of creation. It is no use denying the fact or finding fault with God, it is no use rebelling against it, our only hope is finding the remedy.

JONAH'S DILEMMA

We take you again aboard the ship on which we found Jonah fast asleep. In their desperation, the sailors cast lots to see for whose cause the storm had been loosed upon them, and the lot naturally fell upon Jonah:

> Then said they unto him, Tell us, we pray thee, for whose cause this evil is upon us; What is thine occupation? and whence comest thou? what is thy country? and of what people art thou? (Jonah 1:8).

The cat is finally out of the bag and poor Jonah is forced to confess his sin, and he says,

> I am an Hebrew; and I fear the Lord, the God of heaven, which hath made the sea and the dry land.
> Then were the men exceedingly afraid, and said unto him, Why hast thou done this? For the men knew that he fled from the presence of the Lord, because he had told them (Jonah 1:9, 10).

Poor, poor Jonah. What a mess he had gotten himself into in his backslidden condition and through his disobedience to God. How much easier it would have been for him just to obey since he had to go finally anyway. What fools believers can be when they get away from the Lord and get their eyes off Christ. What trouble they can bring upon themselves and others as well, and what a long hard road it is to come back to the place of fellowship again. We want to be personal and practical in these messages. Are you my friend, living in the will of the Lord? Are you in the place of blessing? Or is your life miserable because you are living contrary to God's will? What is there in your life which is hindering your joy and testimony and making you miserable, sour and unfruitful, and cantankerous? We may find the answer in the story of Jonah.

No Life of Prayer

It is not hard to find the reason for Jonah's predicament. Three things are definitely implied in our Scripture.

1. Jonah had neglected the Word of God.
2. Jonah had neglected his prayer life.
3. Jonah had neglected his testimony.

If the believer is to be a strong and a fruitful Christian, and a power for God, he must observe three inviolable rules.

First, he must feed upon the Word of God. Second, he must live a life of prayer, and third, he must witness for Christ. Neglect of one or the other of these will make a "Jonah" out of any believer. Jonah had neglected the Word of the Lord. He had disobeyed its demands, and instead of going to Nineveh, he had sought to flee from the Lord. He had also neglected his prayer life, for the shipmaster exclaimed:

> What meanest thou, O sleeper? ARISE, CALL UPON THY GOD (Jonah 1:6a).

"Man," the shipmaster seems to say, "why are you not

praying, with the ship floundering about and ready to sink into the depths?"

No Testimony

Then, naturally, the child of God who neglects the Word of God and prayer will have no testimony either. And so it was with Jonah. He had not told them who he was, and so when the lot fell upon him, they showered him with rapid fire questions and said:

> What is thine occupation? and whence comest thou? what is thy country? and of what people art thou? (Jonah 1:8).

And then it is that Jonah had to tell them, but even so, his testimony did not mean a great deal, for his life and his conduct belied his confession. What a lesson this holds for us. If you today are in the place of Jonah, tired, unhappy, defeated, and perhaps chastened of the Lord, examine your own heart for these three things, and you will find that it began with one or more of these three things which you have neglected in your life: the Word of God, prayer and testimony.

You began to neglect your Bible reading and your Bible study, and became lean and weak spiritually. You overslept and rushed off to work without opening God's Word for a single verse of instruction for the day. And naturally, if you were too busy to read your Bible, then you were too busy to pray. Now let us be honest with God and ourselves. Did you read your Bible today? Did you pray before you began the day? Right there you will find the answer to the barrenness in your life and the lack of testimony. And as a result of this, your witness for Christ became silent, and the next thing, in your vulnerable condition, sin crept in, habits took their grip upon you and today you are far, far away from God, miserable, defeated and fruitless.

Honest Confession

If this is your condition, then listen to the story of Jonah. When Jonah was brought face to face with the awful damage he was doing and the judgment he was bringing upon others, he came through with a clear-cut confession:

> And he said unto them, I am an Hebrew; and I fear the Lord, the God of heaven . . .
>
> Then were the men exceedingly afraid, and said unto him, Why hast thou done this? For the men knew that he fled from the presence of the Lord, because he had told them.
>
> Then said they unto him, What shall we do unto thee, that the sea may be calm unto us? for the sea wrought, and was tempestuous (Jonah 1:11).

What a terrible rebuke this was to Jonah, who by his own testimony was a follower of the Lord. The world itself has more sense and better judgment than a backslidden Christian. These mariners knew that something was radically wrong, while Jonah himself was unconscious of it. They had never seen such a storm before in all of their lives, and having found out who was the cause for the tempest, they realized that some action must be taken to make an atonement for this sin if their lives were to be spared.

Throw Me Overboard

Right here the typology of Jonah changes suddenly. Up until this point Jonah is a type of, and represents the guilty sinner because of whom the judgment of death is resting upon the sailors. But now the picture changes entirely. From verse 12 on, Jonah now becomes a type of the Lord Jesus Christ, who took Jonah's and the sinners' place. If the storm is to be stilled, sin must be dealt with, and since the wages of sin is death, the sinner must die. Jonah's death, therefore, is the only thing which can save the sailors from their doom. And so Jonah, by this time thoroughly awakened by the rebuke of the sailors, gives a most strange answer:

> And he said unto them, Take me up, and cast me forth into the sea; so shall the sea be calm unto you: for I know that for my sake this great tempest is upon you (Jonah 1:12).

Cast me forth into the sea! This was God's only way of saving the sailors from their doom. The guilty one must die, for sin must be punished. This is true of the human race. We have sinned and God's judgment is resting upon all of us through Adam's sin and through our personal sin. The sinner, therefore, must die, but instead God wants to save sinners and not destroy them, and so he sent His Son, the Lord Jesus Christ, into the world to take the sinners' place. And by His Death and His Resurrection, He brought peace to the sinner for whom He was willing to die. Jonah, therefore, foreshadows the Lord Jesus Christ. Jonah himself was a sinner, but Christ Himself was sinless. God made Christ to be sin for us that He might take the sinners' place:

> For he hath made him to be sin for us, who knew no sin; that we might be made the righteousness of God in him (II Cor. 5:21).
> The Lord hath laid on him the iniquity of us all (Isa. 53:6b).
> Who his own self bare our sins in his own body on the tree (I Pet. 2:24a).

See here then the clear lesson of the prophet Jonah. One man must die, that many others might have life. This is the great doctrine of substitutionary atonement in the Bible. Caiaphas, the high priest at the trial of the Lord Jesus Christ, stated the matter clearly in John 11:49:

> And one of them, named Caiaphas, being the high priest that same year, saith unto them, Ye know nothing at all.
> Nor consider that it is expedient for us, that one man should die for the people, and that the whole nation perish not.
> And this spake he not of himself: but being high priest that year, he prophesied that Jesus should die for that nation;
> And not for that nation only, but that also he should gather together in one the children of God that were scattered abroad (John 11:49-52).

Because of Adam's sin the world today lies under judgment. But now comes the second Man, the last Adam, the Lord of glory who came to take our place and our sin upon Himself and make it His own personal responsibility. And He, like Jonah, was cast into the sea of God's judgment to die and to rise again for our redemption. The vast world vessel of humanity was plunging through the waves of judgment toward the reefs of eternal doom and destruction because of the sin of man against His God. Soon it would plunge into the abyss or be dashed in pieces upon the jagged rocks of the wrath of a Holy God. There was only one way that the storm, however, could be stilled. The sin question must be settled. Sin must be dealt with and be punished by literal death. Someone must die that others may be saved. And all this is typified by Jonah, the type of our Lord Jesus. He says,

> Take me up, and cast me forth into the sea; so shall the sea be calm unto you (Jonah 1:12).

As Jonah must be thrown overboard to die that the others might live, so the Lord Jesus, the anti-type of the Prophet Jonah, the substitute for Jonah and all sinners like him, must die if they are to live. This was the only remedy, there was no other way.

The sea could not be quieted until Jonah was cast into the deep and God's wrath could not be appeased and His justice satisfied until Jesus had groaned the words upon the Cross, "It is finished." Not till the last sin was paid for, and He voluntarily bowed his head in death could a Holy God be reconciled. But he became our peace, and now:

> . . . being justified by faith, we have peace with God through our Lord Jesus Christ (Rom. 5:1).

We find here in this story of Jonah, therefore, an application for both the saint and the sinner. To those of you who are unsaved, may I ask you a personal question? Have you ever seen this Saviour, the Lord Jesus Christ, as your own personal substitute? Remember that you cannot by the works of your own hands accomplish your own salvation, as we shall see in our coming messages. The sailors tried every device they knew. They cast all of their wares overboard in an effort to lighten the ship and in that way save themselves. Then even after Jonah had told them that he must be cast overboard, they still insisted upon rowing hard, in the hope that they might by their own efforts and by their own labor and by their own works, reach harbor and make the death of the substitute unnecessary. But all of it failed and they had to come to the place where they were willing to accept the death of another if they were to be saved. Do not delay, therefore, but come unto Him now who said that:

He that believeth on him that sent me, hath everlasting life (John 5:24a).

Then, just a word to the Christians. Oh, believer, as we come to the close of this message, I trust that you have appreciated the picture of Christ presented in it all, but until we learn the practical lesson which it has for us personally, individually, we have still missed the important part. We may admire the doctrine taught in the Book of Jonah, and we may subscribe to all of it with a mental assent, but until it becomes practical in our lives and we apply it to our own personal experience, it is all of no avail. We, like Jonah, are God's messengers. If we are saved, we are God's representatives here on the earth to tell the good news of salvation through the Death and Resurrection of Christ. But how many of us, I fear, the majority of God's people, like Jonah, are concerned only with their own needs and spiritual comforts. Yes, you are glad you are saved. You have trusted Christ to be sure, and you can say, "I know whom I have believed." You are happy because you are saved, but what about others round about you? It is days since some of you have talked to a single sinner for Christ. Some of you never witness to others, never give out a tract or visit someone to tell them about the Saviour. While you should be weeping for the lost and repenting of your indifference to the destinies of men round about you, you are making a comfortable bed for yourself in this world. You like Jonah are fast asleep aboard a sinking ship. Christian, may I ask you, therefore, again, do you believe that men and women without the Lord Jesus Christ are destined for a Christless eternity, where there will be nothing but remorse and suffering for those who are cast into outer darkness? Do you realize that you have the only remedy, and that God has committed it to us. He has no other hands but our hands here upon the earth today, and no other mouth but our mouth to tell the story of redeeming grace. May God grant us faithfulness to the commission:

> Go ye into all the world, and preach the gospel to every creature (Mark 16:15).

Chapter Six

THE FUTILITY OF WORKS

And he said unto them, Take me up, and cast me forth into the sea; so shall the sea be calm unto you: for I know that for my sake this great tempest is upon you (Jonah 1:12).

THIS was the voluntary offer of the prophet Jonah. Jonah, we remind you again, is a type of the Lord Jesus Christ in His Death and His Resurrection. This is definitely stated by our Lord Himself in Matthew 12:40 where He said:

For as Jonah was three days and three nights in the whale's belly; so shall the Son of man be three days and three nights in the heart of the earth.

The story of Jonah was a prophecy of the Death and Resurrection of Christ. He is a picture of our Saviour in many, many ways. He was first of all a picture of the Lord Jesus Christ under the judgment of God. He was a picture of God's substitute for sinners who were facing eternal death. He is moreover a type of the Death and the Resurrection of Christ, and finally Jonah becomes a picture of Christ bringing salvation to all the world.

ONE MUST DIE

In our previous message we saw that the only way the storm which threatened the sailors could be calmed, was for Jonah to be cast overboard and to die. There was no other way, there was no alternative. Even so, there is no salvation apart from the Death and Resurrection of the Lord Jesus Christ. But proud and stubborn humanity is slow to believe God's Word. Instead, men seek to save themselves through their own efforts and their own toil and their own works. Man will first exhaust all of his own devices until he is utterly lost, before he will accept God's remedy of grace.

How wonderfully this is illustrated in our narrative. There were two things the sailors tried to do before they would submit to God's command to throw Jonah overboard. The first attempt to save themselves is in Jonah 1:5,

> Then the mariners were afraid, and cried every man unto his god, and cast forth the wares that were in the ship into the sea, to lighten it of them. But Jonah was gone down into the sides of the ship; and he lay, and was fast alseep.

We read that they "cast forth their wares" that were in the ship, into the sea. They thought that by getting rid of their cargo they could outride the storm. They got rid of their impedimenta, but all of their work was of no avail. Even so, foolish man tries to save himself by reformation and giving up things in his own life, and thereby seeking to please God. Men believe that if they will quit lying, stealing, swearing, killing and lusting, and throw these things overboard, they can lighten the ship of their condemnation. This is the way of mere religion. It teaches that if we only give up this and that thing, and live a decent life and join a church, go through religious ceremonies and rituals, we can be made acceptable to God. But all of this was of no avail, for the storm continued unabated.

The second attempt of the sailors to save themselves is found in verse 13. After Jonah had told them plainly that their only hope lay in throwing him overboard, if the storm was to be stilled, we read:

> NEVERTHELESS the men rowed hard to bring it to the land; but they could not: for the sea wrought, and was tempestuous against them (Jonah 1:13).

Nevertheless! This certainly is one big word in the plan of salvation. Nevertheless! It may also be rendered, "In spite of." In spite of Jonah's message they still tried to save themselves, and they "rowed hard," but all of it was of no avail. Their labors were entirely in vain. What unnecessary toil and sweat and tears are wasted in man's effort to save himself by his own works, when the remedy has been given so simply. Man needs first of all to learn the lesson of the futility of his own endeavors before he will cast himself upon the mercy of God, and accept God's only remedy.

LAW AND GRACE

That is why God placed Israel under the law of works. The law was not designed to save man, but to prove that he could NOT save himself. Israel did not feel the need of grace, but the people imagined they could save themselves by their own works of righteousness. And so God gave them the law, and for sixteen hundred years Israel groveled and toiled and groaned under the yoke of the law, only to find that it could not be done and could not be kept. To the demands which Moses transmitted to them from God, Israel had ignorantly and blindly replied:

All that the Lord hath spoken we will do (Ex. 19:8).

Poor, blinded Israel. To God's demands for perfection they answered "all that the Lord hath spoken we will DO." The key to their mistake, of course, is in the word, "DO." They did not realize that fallen man needs the grace of God, and not justice, and so God gave them a law. It was a perfect expression of God's requirements for holiness and perfection. It was a good law, but bad sinners could not keep it. It was a holy law, but unholy sinners were unable to live up to it. It was a perfect law, but imperfect man fell far short of its demands. It was a just law, and therefore, demanded the punishment of its transgressors. And for sixteen hundred years Israel tried to be saved by keeping that law, little realizing that the law could condemn the sinner, but it could not save him. It could demand obedience, but could not pro-

duce obedience. It could tell men how to live, but was powerless to help them live. It could threaten the sinner with death,
but could not save him from death.

WHAT THE LAW COULD NOT DO

We repeat, therefore, that the law was never intended to
save men. God knew when He gave the law that no sinner
would ever keep it. Yea, more, no sinner ever COULD keep
that perfect law. God demanded of Israel something which He
knew Israel was unable to perform. And so for sixteen hundred years of the dispensation of the law, Israel toiled and
labored without one single son of Adam being able to keep it
perfectly or to be justified by its works. And then the people
of Israel ended those sixteen hundred years by murdering the
only Man who ever did keep the law of God perfectly, even
the Lord Jesus Christ.

LAW A SCHOOLMASTER

The law was never intended to save, but to prove and
demonstrate the weakness of the flesh, the total inability of
human nature to measure up to its demands, in order to
bring man to the place where he would admit his total failure,
and cast himself upon the mercy and grace of God. Man must
first be brought to the end of himself, before he will seek
help from God. Paul, looking back over Israel's history, says:

> For by the works of the law shall no flesh be justified (Gal.
> 2:16).

And again:

> For what the law could not do, in that it was weak through
> the flesh, God sending his own Son in the likeness of sinful
> flesh, and for sin, condemned sin in the flesh:
> That the righteousness of the law might be fulfilled IN us,
> who walk not after the flesh, but after the Spirit (Rom. 8:3, 4).

The law was a schoolmaster to teach men their need of
mercy and grace, and to teach them, that by the works of the

law no flesh should be justified in His (God's) sight. And so at the end of the age of testing under the law,

> . . . God sent forth his Son, made of a woman, made under the law,
> To redeem them that were under the law, that we might receive the adoption of sons (Gal. 4:4, 5).

The law acted as a severe schoolmaster or teacher, or pedagogue, to teach man the futility of trying to save himself, and to drive him in faith to the cross of Calvary. Paul asserts this in Galatians 3:24:

> Wherefore the law was our schoolmaster to bring us unto Christ, that we might be justified by faith.
> But after that faith is come, we are no longer under a schoolmaster.
> For ye are all the children of God by faith in Christ Jesus.

OVERBOARD WITH JONAH

This then is the lesson we find graphically illustrated in the story of Jonah. The sailors tried everything in their power to save themselves by their own efforts. But there was only one way they could be saved, and that was not by their own works. Jonah must die! The death penalty must be met and meted out, and so after casting their wares overboard had failed to still the storm, and then toiling and straining at the oars had failed to stop the howling tempest, and they were utterly exhausted, they dropped their oars, ceased their toiling, and cast themselves upon God's mercy. The record is beautiful. After they had labored to the point of utter exhaustion and despair, we then read:

> Wherefore they cried unto the Lord, and said, We beseech thee, O Lord, we beseech thee, let us not perish for this man's life, and lay not upon us innocent blood: for thou, O Lord, hast done as it pleased thee.
> So they took up Jonah, and cast him forth into the sea: and the sea ceased from her raging (Jonah 1:14, 15).

PEACE AT LAST

Peace at last, when they obeyed God's Word. Jonah is cast
overboard into the sea to die, and the sea immediately becomes calm and peaceful. In one moment of time more was
accomplished than hours of toiling, laboring and straining at
the oars. The moment they believed the Word of the Lord
which Jonah had spoken, "Cast me overboard," the struggle
was over. The vicarious death of Jonah meant life for the
trembling sailors. When they ceased struggling, and BELIEVED
God's Word, salvation came in an instant.

This is still God's plan of salvation. Paul tells us in Titus,

> Not by works of righteousness which we have done, but ac-
> cording to his mercy he saved us, by the washing of regen-
> eration, and renewing of the Holy Ghost (Titus 3:5).

Or listen to Paul again, in Romans 4:5,

> But to him that worketh not, but believeth on him that justi-
> fieth the ungodly, his faith is counted for righteousness.

Jonah then becomes a picture of Christ, but only a picture
and a shadow. For Jonah himself was the sinner, while Christ
Himself was sinless. But God laid upon the Lord Jesus Christ
His Son, OUR sin, and so with OUR sin upon Him, He was
able by His death to satisfy the just demands of a holy law,
and bring about eternal salvation to all who would believe.
How slow men have been to grasp this simple plan of salvation. Men still try by all their religious endeavors, good
works, reformation, education, emulation, self-mortification, to
earn their own salvation. Thousands are still deluded by
Satan into believing that if they will "cast their wares overboard" they can still find favor with God. And so they seek
by giving up this, and not doing that, to please God, but
God demands faith in His Son, Jesus Christ, instead. All of
man's efforts to be good, honest, upright, or religious, without
faith in Christ, have no saving value. Of course, there is
virtue in honesty, goodness, charity, and all men are expected
to have these virtues, but as a substitute for the blood of

Christ, they are worthless. There is a remarkable verse in Isaiah 64:6:

> But we are all as an unclean thing and all our righteousnesses are as filthy rags.

Just recently the full impact of that verse seemed to dawn upon me. The Word does not say, "All our overt, wicked sins of lying, stealing, adultery, cursing and wickedness are as filthy rags." No one would dare to deny that. But amazingly it says instead:

> All our RIGHTEOUSNESSES are as filthy rags.

Think of that! The things that we pride ourselves in, our righteous acts are as filthy rags before Almighty God, as a substitute for the blood of Christ. Now I realize that this is a bitter, bitter pill to swallow for the natural man. How often, when we approach people for Christ, they will excuse themselves, and say, "I am not a sinner. I go to church. I live a good life, I pay my debts, I care well for my family, and am kind to dumb animals, and am respected in the community. I give to charity, etc., etc. I think my chances of going to heaven are just as good as anyone's." But listen, my friend, any decent person ought to do all those things which you have mentioned as doing, and they are certainly fine, and we commend them, but without faith they are only as "filthy rags" in the sight of Almighty God, fit only to be cast aside and destroyed. You must be delivered not only from sin, but from the sin of your own self-righteousness. Christ came to save men from two things; from sin, and from religion. And by far the hardest ones to reach are those who are religiously lost.

That is why it is so much easier to lead an overt, open, vile sinner to Christ. We need not convince the harlot, the thief, the robber, the drunkard, that they are sinners and in need of salvation. They know it all too well. But how to reach the self-righteous, respectable, moral, religious and self-satisfied sinner, and show him his need for Christ, is a far more difficult problem. The hardest person to reach with the Gospel is not the down and outer, but the "up and outer." We have missions for "down and outers," but where are the missions for the "up and outers?"

Remember it was to a religious, moral, law-abiding, self-righteous, "up and outer" that Jesus said "Ye must be born again." Have you been hiding behind your own goodness as an excuse for not receiving Christ? Then remember, God looks at all our righteousnesses as filthy rags.

Then a closing word to you who have struggled and toiled to overcome the storm of sin, but have failed. You are the victim of sin and habit, and a slave to iniquity, lust, drunkenness, or whatever it may be. You have resolved again and again to be different. You have vowed over and over again that this was the last time, throwing your wares overboard, only to find that in your own struggle, you only failed again and again. Then listen. Admit that you are helpless and defeated. Admit that you are unable to save yourself and turn to Christ, and like the sailors in Jonah, turn to the Lord God Himself for help and receive His remedy, and experience the truth of the words of II Corinthians 5:17,

> Therefore if any man be in Christ, he is a new creature: old things are passed away; behold, all things are become new.

Chapter Seven

GOD'S USE OF MAN'S WRATH

> So they took up Jonah, and cast him forth into the sea: and
> the sea ceased from her raging (Jonah 1:15).

THE casting overboard of the prophet Jonah is a clear picture
of the death of the Lord Jesus Christ, the Son of God, upon
the Cross of Calvary. Our Lord Himself said in Matthew 12
that Jonah was a picture and a type of His own Death and
Resurrection. The Old Testament is full of shadows, types
and prophetic pictures of the coming Redeemer, but probably
nowhere in the whole realm of Old Testament revelation do
we find a more wonderful and blessed foreshadowing of the
Lord Jesus and His redeeming work than in the Book of
Jonah. We rehearse the story for you again.

Jonah is in a little ship with a mighty tempest threatening
to engulf it, and plunge its occupants into a watery grave.
The angry waves rise up until we read that the ship was
"nigh to be broken." That mighty tempest and the raging
storm may well be taken to represent the righteous wrath
of a holy God against the fallen race of Adam in the frail
ship of this old world system. For mankind as a whole, like
Jonah, has turned its back upon God, and instead of fulfilling
His purpose and obeying His command, is frantically seeking
to lose God, and flees in the opposite direction. Man has
forsaken the mission with which His maker had entrusted
him, and has turned aside to go his own evil way.

57

CHRIST OUR SUBSTITUTE

For this very cause, in order that He might save man from destruction and the storm of eternal wrath into which his self-will had led him, God sent His own Son into the world. He came in the likeness of sinful flesh, though He, unlike Jonah was without sin Himself. He, however, became partaker of our humanity, a sharer of all our weakness and infirmities. He became like any other traveler in the great world ship of humanity, and took His place in the hazardous journey to the rocks of doom. The Bible clearly says that, "He became like unto us in all things, sin only excepted." Like Jonah, He was as much a part of the personnel of the doomed ship as all the rest. He was just as human as we sinners are.

Until the storm threatened to engulf the ship, they counted Jonah as a man of no consequence. They paid but little attention to him as he slept in the hold of the ship. He was of no particular importance to them. Even so, when the Lord Jesus Christ took passage in the boat of human flesh, few recognized the significance of His presence among them, and gave but scant attention to Him. The sailors considered Jonah only another passenger and seemingly ignored him until the storm broke, and then they became aware of his importance, and that only by Jonah's death could they be saved.

Even so when Jesus entered the frail ship of humanity, the people considered him only another man, the Son of a carpenter and the Child of an obscure peasant mother. It made no great stir among them. It is true even today. The great mass of professing Christendom, while it extols His teachings, celebrates His Birthday and Resurrection, sees little more in the Lord Jesus Christ, than just another Man. Yes, a great Man, indeed, but nothing more than just a Man. All this had been prophesied centuries before. The prophet Isaiah had cried out:

> He shall grow up before him as a tender plant, and as a root out of dry ground: he hath no form nor comeliness; and

when we shall see him, there is no beauty that we should desire him.

He is despised and rejected of men; a man of sorrows, and acquainted with grief: and we hid as it were our faces from him; he was despised, and we esteemed him not (Isa. 53:2, 3).

But what tremendous importance was attached to His coming by God the Father. For this very One, the Son of God, held the only key to man's eternal salvation. He Himself must die if we are to live. Only by the Death and Resurrection of Christ can man find redemption. Little did the sailors in the ship realize that Jonah was the key to the stilling of the storm which was threatening their lives. Either Jonah must die or all must be lost. The storm had come because of sin, and sin must be punished by death. And Jesus our Lord became our "Jonah" and our substitute. He took our sin (which was not His own), and bore it to the Cross and made atonement. Of all of this Jonah is a clear type. And now notice the result:

And the sea ceased from her raging (Jonah 1:15).

God Himself had sent the storm in judgment upon sin, and He Himself could calm the storm, but only by removing the cause of the tempest, which was sin. As soon as Jonah was overboard, so soon the storm ceased her raging. The sailors did absolutely nothing except to cast Jonah overboard. Throwing their wares and cargo overboard had failed to still the storm. Rowing hard to make land had proven absolutely futile. They must throw Jonah overboard. Will you notice that Jonah did not jump overboard. He could have done this. He might have said, "I am to blame for this storm, and I will jump into the sea and rid the boat of my presence and the sea will become calm." Ah no, but instead, Jonah says:

Take me up, and cast me forth into the sea (Jonah 1:12).

It must be by their own hands that he is to be offered up by the sailors in death. They must be responsible for Jonah's death. These sailors killed Jonah. With their own hands

they cast him into the waters. And so it was that Jesus our
Sin-bearer, the great anti-type of Jonah, must in the plan
and the program of God, be slain by the very ones who should
benefit by His death. The sailors were guilty of slaying Jonah,
yet by their murder they were saved. This is indeed a mystery,
but no greater mystery than the death of Christ at the hand
of sinners.

WONDERFUL MYSTERY

We stand here before one of the greatest of all great
mysteries in the Word of God. The death of a victim becomes
the means of salvation for the guilty ones who put the victim
to death. God was able to permit wicked men to put the
Saviour to death, and then make that act of murder the means
of saving those who were responsible for His death. We have
this illustrated in many, many passages throughout the Word
of God.

ADAM AND EVE

Take the case of Adam and Eve. God could have made
a man and a woman who could not have sinned. God is
Omnipotent, and He could have done this very thing. Instead, He made them so that they "could" sin if they chose
to. Even then God who is Almighty, could have kept them
from sinning, if He had wanted to. But He did not. God
did not have to place the tree of the knowledge of good and
evil in the Garden where Adam and Eve could have access
to it. He could have kept that tree out of their reach. But
He did not. He permitted man to fall with the resulting
sentence of eternal death.

Yet, out of that fall, God could bring a revelation concerning Himself which would have been impossible (humanly
speaking) had man not fallen. Had sin never entered, we
would never have seen the mercy of God toward sinners.
Had man not fallen, we should never have known the revelation of His grace. Had man not rebelled, there would never

have needed to be a Bible. We would not have the virgin birth, there would have been no Cross, no Resurrection, no need of redemption. We would never be able to sing the song of redemption and of the Lamb.

No Excuse

Now please do not misunderstand what I have said. We have only stated facts. We are not justifying sin on the part of Adam or anyone else. We are not rejoicing in man's fall. We are not minimizing the awfulness of man's rebellion. We are only stating certain facts, facts which we cannot understand, but which are true nevertheless. God was able to take man's sin, and make it the occasion for the exhibition of His love and mercy and grace which only the redeemed can appreciate. Angels who have never been redeemed because they never fell, can never appreciate God's love as we can. They cannot sing redemption's song. They will never know the love and tender mercies of God as we who have been redeemed from the pit can know, and all of this because of our redemption from sin.

The Case of Joseph

Or, take an illustration from the life of Joseph, so well known to all of us. His ten brethren had plotted against him, and had cast him into a dry pit, and then had sold him into the hands of strangers, to be taken into Egypt. This was the end of Joseph as far as his brothers were concerned. They plotted to put him to death, and put him away, and potentially killed their innocent brother. But now notice the astounding result. God could make the sin of Joseph's brethren the means of saving his murderers. For by their rejection of Joseph, he goes to Egypt, and in the time of famine, he saves his wicked brethren from death. Joseph's "potential" death, therefore, was God's way of saving the lives of those who had put him to death and plotted against him. God was able to take their sin and make it the occasion for saving the wicked sinners. Joseph reminded his brethren of this many, many years later, when in referring to their crime, he says:

> But as for you, ye thought evil against me; but God meant it unto good, to bring to pass, as it is this day, to save much people alive (Gen. 50:20).

God meant it unto good—to save much people alive. Mystery of mysteries. God causes the wrath of man to praise Him. Adam's sin brings into bold relief the love and the mercy and the grace of God. The sin of Joseph's brethren was the occasion for God's plan to save the house of Jacob alive.

AT CALVARY

But as a climaxing illustration of all of this, we must stand finally before the Cross of Calvary. There upon the Cross hangs the Son of God, sinless, perfect, holy, undefiled, and separate from sinners. And yet, there He hangs. He had done no evil. The last verdict was, "I find no fault in him." And around that Cross swarms a milling, howling, bloodthirsty mob of murderers, thirsting for the blood of this innocent Man. Now will you please remember that you and I are represented in that mob. It is OUR sin which nailed Him to the Cross of Calvary.

> It was for crimes that we had done,
> He groaned upon the Tree.
> Amazing pity, grace unknown,
> And love beyond degree.

Will you remember that:

> He was wounded for our transgressions, he was bruised for our iniquities: the chastisement of our peace was upon him; and with his stripes we are healed (Isa. 53:5).

Yet, there He hangs in desperation and suffering while the sadistic mob shrieks out in glee at His suffering, and taunts Him with the cruelest dart of all:

> He saved others; let him save himself, if he be Christ, the chosen of God (Luke 23:35).

How little they knew that if He saved Himself they would have to be forever lost. Then comes the acme of His suffering. An untimely night falls upon the earth, as God turns His back upon His own Son, snuffs out the lights of heaven, and pulls down the curtains of the sky, and forsakes Him utterly as He cries out:

My God, my God, why hast thou forsaken me? (Mark 15:34).

But to this cry there is no answer. All is silent. There is no answer from heaven. My God, we ask, why don't You do something? My God, how can You suffer this vicious murder of an innocent One to go on without interference. Oh, God, why not send fire from heaven, and damn the wicked mob and plunge them into the eternal hell forever. That would be only just and right for God to do. No one could raise a voice in opposition.

GOD'S ANSWER

But listen! God could do something greater than damn these murderers and plunge them in justice into perdition for the death of His Son. He could silently permit them to murder His Son, and then make that death the means of salvation for those who murdered Him. And that is just what God did. He permitted the death of His own Son at the hands of sinners, in order that by His death He might save those who put Him to death. I confess that I cannot understand this mystery. I can only stand in wonder and awe and amazement, and cry out, "My Lord, and my God."

All of this we believe was foreshadowed by the case of Jonah. He must die that the ship and its crew might be saved. But listen, they must cast him overboard, with their own hands. They must accept the responsibility for his death as their substitute, and that is God's plan of salvation today. You too, my dear friend, must personally accept the Death and Resurrection of Christ as your own salvation, as your only hope of redemption, looking away from all of your own efforts, and all of your own works, and all of your own struggles. You must come to the place where you are utterly defeated and admit that your sin drove Him to the Cross and realize that only by the provision which God has made in the Person of the Lord Jesus Christ can you be saved.

> Believe on the Lord Jesus Christ and thou shalt be saved, and thy house (Acts 16:31).

Chapter Eight

THE JUDGMENT OF BELIEVERS

> So they took up Jonah, and cast him forth into the sea: and the sea ceased from her raging.
>
> Then the men feared the Lord exceedingly, and offered a sacrifice unto the Lord, and made vows (Jonah 1:15, 16).

THE death of Jonah meant life for the sailors in the ship. The story of the death and resurrection of Jonah is the story of the Gospel, for Jesus Himself asserts in Matthew 12:

> For as Jonas was three days and three nights in the whale's belly; so shall the Son of man be three days and three nights in the heart of the earth (Matt. 12:40).

In our previous studies we have pointed out repeatedly the central lesson in the first chapter of Jonah; namely, that Jonah must die if the sailors were to live. It was only after the sailors had exhausted every other effort to save themselves that they obeyed God's command, and accepted Jonah's death as their only hope of salvation. Only when these men were willing to acknowledge their own inability to save themselves, and to take God's remedy, could they be saved.

PLAN IS STILL THE SAME

That picture of the plan of God's salvation has never changed. As long as man seeks to save himself, he is lost. God will accept no help from man in His work of redemption. He will not share the glory of salvation with a creature, for "Salvation is of the Lord." Jonah also found this out (Jonah 2:9). God will not do His work of salvation for the sinner

until the sinner has ceased working himself. How clearly
Paul states it in Romans 4:5,

> But to him that worketh not, but believeth on him that
> justifieth the ungodly, his faith is counted for righteousness.

When, therefore, the sailors had come to the end of their
wits, and cast the prophet overboard, suddenly the sea became
calm, and they were safe. This startling experience had its
effect upon these men, for they began to offer sacrifices and
made vows to the Lord. This was the fruit of their experience
and their faith. But notice, they were not saved because they
offered sacrifices, but they sacrificed because they had been
saved. Works are not in payment for salvation, but they are
the fruit of salvation. Their sacrifice could not have stilled
the storm. Another must be sacrificed in their place, and so,
in gratitude and thanksgiving to God these men sacrificed
unto the Lord.

But notice further, that they vowed vows. They made
promises to Almighty God who had saved them. They were
not saved because they had promised God something, but
after they had been saved, they promised their obedience to
the Lord. Their salvation was all of grace through the death
of another, and then the works naturally followed. Their
sacrifices and vows were not the basis for their salvation,
but the normal fruit of their salvation.

Saved By Grace

We, too, do not work for our salvation, but we do work
because we have been saved. The apostle Paul says in Philip-
pians:

> Work out your own salvation with fear and trembling.
> For it is God which worketh in you both to will and to do of
> his good pleasure (Phil. 2:12, 13).

This verse has been grossly misunderstood and misinter-
preted by the legalists who would add works to the plan of
salvation. The verse does NOT SAY, "Work FOR your salvation,"

but it says definitely "work OUT your own salvation." God works salvation IN, and then we are to work it OUT. You cannot work anything OUT until it has first of all been worked IN by God. And so Paul adds:

> For it is God which worketh in you both to will and to do of his good pleasure (Phil. 2:13).

AN ILLUSTRATION

Suppose someone gives me a piece of land as a free gift. I receive a warranty deed to the property with no strings attached. It is mine. I did not work for it, I paid nothing for it, I did nothing to obtain it. But now I do have a responsibility, having received this parcel of land as a free gift. I can now cultivate it, or I can neglect it. The donor of the property now expects and desires of me that in gratitude I shall work the land, keep the buildings in good repair, produce a maximum crop of fruit, and that means WORK. I am not "working" to purchase the land, but working OUT that which I have already received, and then when the harvest comes, with my hands filled with fruit, I joyfully present the results of my labor to him as an act of gratitude and thankfulness and appreciation for his great kindness, and not in an effort to pay him for the gift.

The believer is saved by grace, and grace alone, but this very fact places him under a tremendous responsibility. The Lord has saved us to serve, to work, to produce fruit, and to produce a maximum of fruit, for there is a harvest coming, and a day of reckoning when we shall give an account before our Master. We shall be called into account as to what we have done for Him who gave His all for us, and what we have done with the salvation which He has purchased for us, and given to us by His grace. The Bible clearly teaches that there is a judgment seat of Christ, when the Lord will reward each one of us on the record of our works, after we have been saved. Paul in II Corinthians 5:10 says:

> For we must all appear before the judgment seat of Christ;
> that every one may receive the things done in his body, accord-
> ing to that he hath done, whether it be good or bad.

This judgment has nothing to do with salvation. It is not
to be confused with the judgment of the Great White Throne
in Revelation 20. There only the wicked will appear. But at
the judgment seat of Christ, which will take place immediately
after the rapture, only born-again believers will be present.
Their salvation will not be at stake and the matter of their
sin will not be the issue at that time. That was forever settled
when they received the Lord Jesus Christ by faith and were
justified in His sight. But their position in the Kingdom and
the reign with Christ will depend upon the record of their
works. Listen to Paul in I Corinthians:

> For other foundation can no man lay than that is laid, which
> is Jesus Christ (I Cor. 3:11).

To build on that foundation is to have eternal life. It can
never be lost, because it is the free gift of God by grace, and
we have done nothing to obtain it. But that is not the whole
story. Someone will say, "If this be true, and we have eternal
life, then we can live as we please and do as we want to,
and go to heaven just the same at the end of the road." Listen,
my friend, anyone who talks thus, is still ignorant of the grace
of God and the Word of God. Paul, therefore, adds in I
Corinthians 3:12, 13:

> Now if any man build upon this foundation gold, silver,
> precious stones, wood, hay, stubble;
> Every man's work shall be made manifest: for the day shall
> declare it, because it shall be revealed by fire; and the fire shall
> try every man's work of what sort it is.

These words were spoken to believers, to born-again saints
who are building upon the one foundation, and are secure in
their salvation. But in spite of this, God is going to call
them into account at the end, as to what they have done
WITH that which was entrusted to their care.

There are two groups of materials mentioned in this passage on the judgment seat. First of all, you will notice that we have gold, silver and precious stones. That is one group. These are products of a creative act, imperishable, and not the result of natural growth. Precious stones may be small, but valuable. They are not injured by passing through the fire. They represent the fruit of the spirit, the result of the new nature in Christ Jesus. However, the other group is in sharp contrast to precious stones, and is composed of wood, hay and stubble, which are not the result of a creative act, but the result of a natural process of growth and development. They represent the things of the flesh and our old nature. They may be bulky, but they are worthless. They are perishable, and will all go up in smoke at the judgment seat of Christ.

WHAT IS YOUR SCORE?

How much of your Christian service is spiritual, and how much of it is carnal? We ought to ask ourselves these questions before we stand in account before Him. Is my service only for my personal satisfaction, or is it a loving sacrifice in appreciation of His salvation which counts not the cost to itself, but seeks only to glorify God? Do I preach to please God, or to receive the praise of men? Do I preach out of a heart of love for God and my fellowmen and for lost sinners, or only for my own profit and satisfaction? Is it to please men, or is it to please God? That is the question that ought to determine our action before Him. Is it "gold, silver and precious stones," or only "wood, hay and stubble?"

Do you sing because you love to tell His praises, or because you want people to admire your beautiful voice? Do you work in the church for the admiration of others, or for the glory of God? There will be some big bonfires at the judgment seat of Christ, when everything done for personal reasons and selfish purposes will perish in the flames. May God help us to weigh all we do in this balance of the judgment seat of

Christ, before we stand before Him. Then, listen to the rest of the story:

> If any man's work abide which he hath built thereupon, he shall receive a reward.
>
> If any man's work shall be burned, he shall suffer loss: but he himself shall be saved; yet so as by fire (I Cor. 3:14, 15).

SOLEMN WORDS

Certainly these are solemn words, spoken as they are to believers who have been redeemed by the precious blood of the Lord Jesus Christ, and through God's grace. This is not spoken to unbelievers, for Paul emphatically states:

> He himself shall be saved; yet so as by fire (I Cor. 3:15).

There will be some believers who at the end of the road will be saved, "yet so as by fire." I do not know just what is meant by the "fire" in these verses. I am not prepared to say whether it refers to literal fire, or whether it is only a figure of speech, but one thing I do know, whichever it may be, it will not be a pleasant experience for those who have wasted their opportunities and their talents here below. The text says, "He shall suffer loss." It does not say, "he shall enjoy loss." Let me again remind you, it does not say the believer shall be burned, but his WORKS shall all perish, "saved so as by fire."

We have but to think of the experience of Lot. Lot was a believer but a carnal, worldly, fleshly believer. One would never suppose from the record in Genesis that Lot even knew the Lord or that he was a believer, but the New Testament definitely tells us that Lot was a believer, and that he was a follower of the Lord (II Peter 2:7, 8). It was for this reason that he was saved from the destruction of Sodom, while all the rest of the sinners perished in the flames. Yes, Lot was saved from the judgment of Sodom, but what a salvation it turned out to be. He lost everything in the fire but his life, and escaped with the smell of brimstone upon his very garments.

Just because we have been saved by the grace of God, therefore, does not give us a license to rest upon our oars, or to spend our life merely enjoying our salvation for ourselves, but to recognize the fact that we have a job to do, a responsibility to meet, and a Lord to whom we shall have to give an account. Salvation by grace, therefore, becomes the most impelling motive in all the world for living a life of godliness and separation, holiness and purity. What regret there will be at the judgment seat of Christ when we look back and see the opportunities that have been lost, and we shall have to take an inferior position in the Kingdom of our Lord's glorious reign, just because we have built upon the foundation, "hay, wood, and stubble." Paul tells us definitely in Titus that the motive for our godliness and for holiness in life and for productiveness in service is the fact that we have been saved by grace. Any man, therefore, who makes the matter of grace an occasion for carelessness, still does not know the grace of God. Paul in writing to Titus, the young preacher, says:

> For the grace of God that bringeth salvation hath appeared to all men,
> Teaching us that, denying ungodliness and worldly lusts, we should live soberly, righteously, and godly, in this present world;
> Looking for that blessed hope, and the glorious appearing of the great God and our Saviour Jesus Christ;
> Who gave himself for us, that he might redeem us from all iniquity, and purify unto himself a peculiar people, zealous of good works (Titus 2:11-14).

You will notice from this that it is the grace of God that teaches us, (1) negatively, to deny all ungodliness and worldly lusts, and (2) positively, that Christ will purify us for Himself a peculiar people, zealous of good works. If there are no good works as a result of your salvation, you have a perfect right to doubt whether you have ever been saved by the grace of God.

Will you, therefore, right now examine your own heart for

anything which you know is displeasing to the Lord, and which you would not want to be present when you are called into account before Him. Would you welcome Jesus to come right at this moment? Is there anything in your life that you would want to get rid of before you meet Him? Then remember that one of these days, the Lord is going to come, and if you are living a careless life, it will be for you not the blessed experience of joy and happiness, but to be ashamed at His appearing.

The sailors in the case of Jonah proved their faith by their good works, and after they had been saved and the sea had been made calm, they,

> . . . feared the Lord exceedingly, and offered a sacrifice unto the Lord, and made vows (Jonah 1:16).

Chapter Nine

THE GREAT COMMISSION IN JONAH

> Now the Lord had prepared a great fish to swallow up Jonah.
> And Jonah was in the belly of the fish three days and three
> nights (Jonah 1:17).

WHEN a dog bites a man, that is not news; but when a man
bites a dog, that is news. In the same way, when a man
catches a fish, that is not news; but when a fish catches a man,
that IS news. Most people, however, accept almost all fish
stories with a couple of teaspoons of salt, for fishermen from
time immemorial have been proverbial prevaricators. Most
people, therefore, quite naturally discount all fish stories. This
may even have some psychological bearing upon the fact that
skeptics and unbelievers also discount the fishing reports
of the Bible. For there are many accounts of fishing in the
Scriptures. Most of the disciples were fishermen, and Jesus
accompanied them many times, and became responsible for a
number of amazing and miraculous catches.

JONAH TOPS THEM ALL

But the best known and by far the most striking of all the
accounts of fishing in the Bible is the record of Jonah, the
prophet of the Lord, who spent three days and three nights
in the belly of a fish, came forth alive and well, and became
the great preacher of repentance to the wicked city of Nineveh.
But the most amazing thing about Jonah's experience is that
it is true. This record is told, not by man, but by God, so that
it positively precludes all untruthfulness and exaggeration.
God cannot lie, and the Holy Spirit who inspired the author

73

of Jonah to write this account cannot lie. Moreover Jesus Himself vouches for the truthfulness and historicity of the story in Matthew 12.

And yet no book has been the butt of so much ridicule as the Book of Jonah. The average man passes it off as mere fiction, while a few well-meaning but misguided champions of the inspiration of the Bible seek high and low, turn heaven and earth upside down in a search for a fish which actually could swallow a man, and keep him alive. Periodically, some well-meaning, self-appointed defender of the Bible comes up with reports and discoveries of some strange sea animal washed ashore on some beach which has a throat large enough to swallow a man without crushing him, and a stomach so spacious it could contain sufficient air to furnish oxygen enough to sustain a man for several days. Thus men try to vindicate God in the account of Jonah.

If such an animal could be found, it would still prove nothing. We believe the story of Jonah because it is God's Word, and not because it can be scientifically proven. The whole story of Jonah is a succession of miracles, as illustrating the greater miracle of the Death and the Resurrection of the Lord Jesus Christ. If it could be proven that there is a fish large enough to swallow a man, with enough gas on its stomach to keep a person in oxygen for days, and so devoid of gastric juice that it could not digest such a tender morsel as a fleeing prophet, it would destroy the entire story, and discredit the whole Gospel of the Death and Resurrection. It must be received by faith, for it is a miracle. Remove the miraculous from Jonah and you destroy the Gospel of the Death and Resurrection of Christ.

FAITH IN JONAH ESSENTIAL

We, therefore, repeat that faith in the literal account of Jonah is indispensable to salvation. To deny the story of Jonah as a literal record is to deny the literal Death and Resurrection of Christ. We continue to emphasize the words of the Lord Jesus, "As Jonah . . . so the Son of man." If Jonah is fiction, then so is Christ, and also the Resurrection of the Lord Jesus Christ.

We emphasize this point because it is basic and fundamental and essential. All this searching for proof of the possibility of man staying alive in a fish's belly is evidence that we do not consider the simple record of the Bible sufficient, but we need some additional proof. It is a denial of faith, a slur upon the absolute finality and truthfulness of God's Word. God expects us to believe what He says by faith. God's Word needs no proof. It can stand on its own record.

WHAT SAY THE SCRIPTURES

The record of the Book is our only absolute authority. Our Scripture says that God had prepared a great fish to swallow Jonah. The Bible does not reveal the particular species of this fish, but we know that it was a fish, and not a whale. A whale is a mammal which has lungs and breathes air through its nostrils or vents leading to its lungs. But a fish does not breathe air directly for it has no lungs, but takes the oxygen from the water through its gills. This creature which swallowed Jonah was a fish and not a whale. The identical word used throughout the Old Testament for "fish" is used here and not the word for whale. This makes the whole story still more miraculous and outside the realm of naturalistic explanation.

But someone will remind me that Jesus called it a "whale" in Matthew 12, and says, "As Jonah was in the whale's belly." But the word in the Greek is "ketos," and my lexicon defines it as a huge fish, and NOT A WHALE. It was some sort of a fish, big enough to swallow up Jonah. But notice that the search by science for the fish is quite futile, and men never will be able to find one like it, for it was a specially prepared fish which God furnished for this particular occasion.

Notice the words:

> Now the Lord had PREPARED a great fish to swallow up Jonah (Jonah 1:17).

It was a specially prepared fish, and presumably God made it just for this occasion, because there was no other existing fish which would serve the purpose. If there had been a fish in existence that could do the work of swallowing Jonah and keep him alive, then why did God have to prepare one especially for this purpose? But the Bible says that God specially prepared this fish. It was easy for God to do so. He it was Who made the worlds and the universe. He it was who populated the seas in the first place, and created the fishes. Is it then too wonderful to believe that He could do it again? This fish according to the Book was prepared by the Lord specifically for Jonah. Now that may mean either one of two things. Either the Lord took a then existing fish and made it fit for the task that He had assigned to it, or He made a completely new fish for the purpose. What after all is the difference as long as the Omnipotent God is doing it? In the first instance, He could have dilated the fish's throat without inconvenience to the fish, and after Jonah got in there, surely God could preserve him by a miracle from the destructive gastric juices which under natural conditions would have completely digested the victim in less than eighteen hours.

MANY MIRACLES IN JONAH

But this is only one of many miracles in Jonah. The terrible storm which God sent upon the sea was a miracle. The fact the storm was stilled the moment Jonah was cast overboard was a miracle. The fact that God prepared a great fish was a miracle, and the fact that the fish was right where Jonah fell in was also a miracle. Why, oh, why, then do men object to the miracle of the fish swallowing a man? The fact that the fish vomited up Jonah on dry land was a miracle. The fact that he suffered no ill was a miracle. Later on, the growing of a gourd overnight was a miracle, as the coming of the worm to destroy the gourd, and the east wind which followed, all were miraculous.

THE PRACTICAL LESSON

So we would like to point out the glorious truth as suggested by the verse with which we opened this message. It is suggested by the phrase, "Now God had prepared." Yes, God was prepared for the emergency in which His erring prophet found himself because of his disobedience. God had prepared a great fish. Before Jonah was cast overboard God had already made arrangements for his unsolicited reception. He had a room all ready for him, awaiting his occupancy. It certainly was a strange reception in a strange place, but it was God's place for Jonah. Had the fish not been there, Jonah would have drowned. God is always, therefore, prepared for every emergency, even when we are seeking to flee away from the Lord.

Jonah could not get beyond the care of God. He tried to run away, but God followed him. He tried to forget about it and fell fast asleep, but God awakened him. He said, "Cast me overboard for my sin and destroy me," but God had a different plan for Jonah, not his destruction, but his life. So God brought him back from death into His service. To be sure, it was a painful way and a dreadful experience, but it was God's way of teaching Jonah the lesson which he needed to learn. How much better if he had only been willing to be obedient to the Lord in the first place. He could have prevented all of this inconvenience. It would have saved him all of this dreadful experience.

God has also given to us a commission, just as He gave to Jonah. To Jonah He said:

> Arise, go to Nineveh, that great city, and preach unto it the preaching that I bid thee (Jonah 1:2).

But to us He has said:

> Go ye into all the world, and preach the gospel to every creature (Mark 16:15).

We are as much God's messengers as Jonah ever was. We are His representatives in this dispensation to tell the news of redemption to a lost world. The same message which Jonah had to bring, is the message which we have to bring. Jonah's experience in the fish's belly as illustrating the Death and Resurrrection of the Lord Jesus Christ is still the message which we are to bring, telling men and women that while they were unable to save themselves, God by sending His Son to the Cross of Calvary and raising Him from the dead, has made justification and salvation possible to all who will believe. But instead, too many of us, like Jonah, have not heeded God's call. Some of you never witness to others. While we should be weeping over lost souls and repenting of our indifferences and laxity and laziness, we are smug and comfortable in our religious apathy, when we ought to be on fire for God. May I, therefore, ask you, before we come to the close of this particular message, Do you believe that men and women about you are lost by nature, and without Christ are destined to an eternal hell? Do you believe the message of judgment which the Lord gives to all those who die without faith in Christ? I want to press the question home. Do we believe it? If we don't, then we have nothing more to say, but if you are a Bible-believing, born-again Christian, then you must believe that men are lost without the Lord Jesus Christ. And believing that, we also know that only Jesus Christ can save men and women from eternal doom. Do we really actually believe that, or is it just a matter of our confession? If it is something we actually believe, and we look upon our fellow men as those who are on the way to eternal doom, then why have we not told them about the glad message of salvation? What would you think of me if I, a physician, lived in a city where thousands were dying from a dread disease, and I had a remedy which had never been known to fail? Suppose I had an unlimited supply of that remedy, but instead of offering and bringing it to the dying, I just rejoice in the fact that it had cured me, and then just sit around with my precious remedy, rejoicing in my own health, while the multitudes round about me are dying. What would you say of me? Never mind, I know just exactly what you would say.

But, listen, Christian. About you today are multitudes in worse than physical danger. They are in danger of eternal death. You and I have the remedy for a lost world in the Gospel of the Lord Jesus Christ, and yet we must confess that we have not offered it as freely and as earnestly as we should have done. Oh, may we promise God right now that from this day on, we will seek to bring the Gospel remedy to just as many as we possibly can in the days that still are ours for witnessing. God has so ordered that by the preaching of the Gospel men shall be saved, and He has committed this preaching to sinners saved by grace. May God help us to be more earnest, yea, as dead in earnest as Jesus was when He suffered the shameful death upon the Cross that you and I might be saved.

Oh, that the Lord might grip us with the consciousness that we have a personal responsibility. There are some things which cannot be done by proxy. God expects of each one of us, that we should do our part as the opportunity is given to us, and as He lays it upon our hearts. May we heed the words of that old hymn we used to sing so much in days gone by:

> Rescue the perishing, care for the dying;
> Snatch them in pity from sin and the grave.
> Weep O'er the erring one, lift up the fallen,
> Tell them of Jesus, the Mighty to save.

Chapter Ten

THE GOSPEL ACCORDING TO JONAH

> Then Jonah prayed unto the Lord his God out of the fish's belly,
>
> And said, I cried by reason of mine affliction unto the Lord, and he heard me; out of the belly of hell cried I, and thou heardest my voice (Jonah 2:1, 2).

WHEN the prophet Jonah was cast into the sea and was swallowed by a great fish, he became a clear type of the Death and Resurrection of the Lord Jesus Christ. The miracle in Jonah is not that he remained alive in the belly of the fish for three days, but the miracle in Jonah is far greater; namely, that Jonah died, and after three days and three nights arose from his grave in the belly of the fish, and became the preacher of the Gospel to the Gentiles. All of the efforts, therefore, to prove the possibility of a man surviving Jonah's ordeal without dying are entirely without point or purpose, and a waste of valuable time and effort. There is not one single hint in the entire record that Jonah remained alive in the belly of the fish. This has been carried over by sheer tradition. Instead, the entire record clearly teaches that Jonah died and was resurrected, and thus only could become a type of the Death and Resurrection of the Lord Jesus Christ.

JONAH IN SHEOL

That Jonah died is definitely stated in our Scripture. In Jonah 2:1 Jonah prays from the belly of the fish, but in verse 2 he prays from the belly of hell. Notice carefully the inspired words:

> I cried by reason of mine affliction unto the Lord . . .
> out of the belly of hell cried I (Jonah 2:2).

In verse one Jonah is in the belly of the fish, but in verse two he is in the belly of hell (*sheol*).

Now these two places are not the same, or the Holy Spirit would have used the same word in both instances. When Jonah cried in verse one it was immediately after he had been swallowed, and he was still alive and conscious. But he did not survive for long, for soon after, he had this testimony:

> Out of the belly of *sheol* cried I (Jonah 2:2).

We call your attention to the use of two different words translated "belly" in these two verses. The first use of the word, "belly" (of the fish) in verse one is *me-ah* in the original language, and means literally "an abdomen." But the second time the word, "belly" occurs in Jonah 2:2, quite another word is used. It is *betan* and means "a hollow place." literally, therefore, verse one should read:

> Jonah prayed unto the Lord his God out of the fish's abdomen (Jonah 2:1).

But in verse two we should literally read:

> Out of the hollow place of *sheol* cried I (Jonah 2:2).

The spirit of God in dictating this record through Jonah had a purpose in using two entirely different words, to describe two entirely different places from which Jonah prayed. And right here we must state that the word translated "hell" is *sheol* in the Hebrew. *Sheol* in the Old Testament, invariably and without a single exception, is used to describe the place of the departed spirits of those who have died. There are no exceptions to this rule, unless the case of Jonah be one. *Sheol* is the place where the souls of men went upon death, before the coming of the Lord Jesus Christ and His Resurrection. Of the scores of times in which the word *sheol*, and its Greek equivalent, *hades*, are used in the Bible, it always and invariably refers to only one thing, the place of the departed dead.

FAULTY TRANSLATION

It is indeed regrettable that the translators of our King James Version have overlooked this important fact, and have variously translated *sheol* and *hades* as "hell" and "grave" and "pit." This has been corrected in the Revised Version, but in the King James Version this failure has been the source of a great deal of confusion and misunderstanding. The soul of Jonah, therefore, went into *sheol,* while his body rested in death in the abdomen of the fish. This place called *sheol,* is located, according to this chapter, down at "the bottoms (roots) of the mountains" (Jonah 2:6). This is in perfect harmony with every other passage of the Bible dealing with *sheol-hades.*

Because Jonah went to *sheol* and Christ also descended into *sheol,* we want to consider the Bible teaching concerning this place of the departed souls of men. We feel it imperative and highly necessary to do so, because of the widespread ignorance of this aspect of Bible revelation, and the capital which has been made of this misunderstanding by those who would lead us astray.

WHAT IS SHEOL OR HADES?

Two words are used to describe the place of the dead; one in the Old Testament and one in the New Testament. The Hebrew word is *sheol,* and the Greek word so translated is *hades.* This is the word translated "hell" in Jonah 2:2. The Lord Jesus Christ Himself gave us the most complete and clear picture of this place. In the Gospel through Luke we read:

> There was a certain rich man, which was clothed in purple and fine linen, and fared sumptuously every day:
> And there was a certain beggar named Lazarus, which was laid at his gate, full of sores,
> And desiring to be fed with the crumbs which fell from the rich man's table: moreover the dogs came and licked his sores.
> And it came to pass, that the beggar died, and was carried

by the angels into Abraham's bosom: the rich man also died, and was buried;

And in hell (hades) he lift up his eyes, being in torments, and seeth Abraham afar off, and Lazarus in his bosom.

And he cried and said, Father Abraham, have mercy on me, and send Lazarus, that he may dip the tip of his finger in water, and cool my tongue; for I am tormented in this flame.

But Abraham said, Son, remember that thou in thy lifetime receivedst thy good things, and likewise Lazarus evil things: but now he is comforted, and thou art tormented.

And beside all this, between us and you there is a great gulf fixed: so that they which would pass from hence to you cannot; neither can they pass to us, that would come from thence.

Then he said, I pray thee therefore, father, that thou wouldest send him to my father's house:

For I have five brethren; that he may testify unto them, lest they also come into this place of torment.

Abraham saith unto him, They have Moses and the prophets: let them hear them (Luke 16:19-29).

Now we have quoted at length the entire passage so that we may have the picture clearly before us. You have probably noticed that in quoting this passage spoken by the Lord Jesus that we substituted the word, *hades,* for the word "hell." If you have a Revised Version, you will notice that it is thus translated. The word is not "hell," but *hades,* the word for the temporary abode of the souls of the departed. It is, as we have already pointed out, the same as *sheol* in the Old Testament, and always has this same meaning. This narrative, therefore, has been for some, a difficult one to explain, especially for those who would have us believe in annihilation, and soul sleeping. Although the record is so clear, and the evidence so conclusive, coming from the lips of our Lord, nevertheless, men have tried in every way possible to get rid of the passage or else by distorting it, make it mean something other than the clear teaching set forth. One of the most common attempts to get rid of Christ's teaching concerning the place of torment for the wicked in *sheol-hades* is by making this narrative a parable, and then spiritualizing the truth entirely away. Notice, therefore, that this story of the rich man and Lazarus is NOT a parable. It is neither called a parable, nor is its structure such as would suggest its parabolic teaching. It is an actual historical record of two men who lived and died and found themselves after death in the place described as, on the one hand, a place of torment, and on the other hand, a place of comfort in the bosom of Abraham. There is not one single thing in the entire story to even suggest that it is a parable. Where and when the Lord Jesus spake in parables, He always made it clear that His speech was parabolic, and was not to be taken literally. Either it is called a parable as in the chapter preceding this one (Luke 15) in the parable of the sheep, the coin, or else the language is such that it is implied that it is a parable. This then is an actual description of the place of the departed dead at the time Jesus spake these words. And will you notice first of all that both the rich man and Lazarus went to the same general place. They could see each other, they could converse with one another. But still they were separated, and their condition was totally different, for Lazarus was in a place of rest and comfort, while the rich man was tormented in the flame. This place called *hades* was divided into two separate compartments, one for the wicked dead, and one for the saved. Between these two compartments was a great gulf fixed which no one could cross. On the one side are the saved, in peace and bliss and happiness in Abraham's bosom. On the other side are the lost, in torment.

THE PLACE OF THE DAMNED

First of all, therefore, notice Jesus' description of the lost in *sheol-hades*. He plainly tells us that the souls of men are conscious after death. Lazarus died and was carried by angels into Abraham's bosom. It would be absurd to carry a dead, sleeping soul into this place. Of the rich man also, it is said that he died and was buried. Of course, it was his body which was being buried, for we cannot bury a soul, and so Jesus said that the body was buried, but the rich man himself "lifted his eyes up in *sheol-hades*," and saw Lazarus afar off. He was not asleep, but was awake. He saw Lazarus and Abraham, and he talked with them (not in his sleep). If there were no other revelation in the entire Bible, this alone would put to silence the doctrine of "soul sleeping" after death. Even if someone insists that this is a parable, it still does not change the teaching of the Lord Jesus Christ. Certainly our Saviour, even in parabolic language, would not teach something which was not absolutely true, and so we rest the case entirely upon the authority of our Lord, that after death the souls of men remain conscious. This too is taught in the record of Jonah. He is said to cry out of the belly of *sheol*. He was conscious after death, for unconscious souls cannot pray. Jonah was conscious in *sheol*.

PLACE OF MEMORY

Moreover it was a place of memory. This rich man remembered the poor fellow who had lain at his gate begging. He remembered that he had five brothers who were not saved, and now when it was too late, he was concerned about them. It was a place of keen recognition, and an evidence that the souls of the departed remember clearly their past sojourn here upon the earth. Abraham had died many years before Moses and the prophets, but the rich man knew about them just the same. He mentions them and their testimony. Yes, indeed, there is not only consciousness and memory after death, but a knowledge of some things at least which are happening here upon the earth.

PLACE OF REMORSE

Notice further that it was a place, and not merely a condition. The rich man pleads with Abraham to warn his brethren, lest they come into this PLACE of torment and he is filled with remorse at being there, not only for himself, but remorse at not having warned his family. Moreover it was a place of eternal torment. There is no crossing over, and there is no getting out. Abraham makes this clear, that no one can come from either side to the other, for the gulf between them is fixed. It also refutes the teaching that there is any communication between the dead and the living. Our newspapers recently printed a story of a great magician's widow who had waited for years for word from her departed husband, but none had ever come. Well, Jesus teaches that definitely here. While there is communication "among" the dead, it is impossible for the dead to communicate with the living, or the living with the dead.

It is, therefore, evident from the teaching of the Scriptures generally, and from this passage in Luke 16 particularly, that death does not end all, but rather, the Bible says.

> It is appointed unto men once to die, but AFTER THIS the judgment (Heb. 9:27).

Certainly if death meant the cessation of existence, there would be no point whatsoever in judging "dead" people. The soul must be alive to be judged, and we believe that the future judgment will take place in a resurrected body to which the soul which has never died has been restored. To go into eternity, therefore, without Christ will find you with the rich man in the place of eternal doom and outer darkness. But to those who receive the Lord Jesus Christ there is only glory by and by. The way has been made perfectly plain in the Scriptures. We are but to face the fact that we are going to spend eternity somewhere, face the fact that we are lost and cannot save ourselves, and then believe God's own word, and come by faith to the Lord Jesus Christ, accept His finished work, and trust Him Who said,

> Whosoever shall call upon the name of the Lord shall be saved (Rom. 10:13).

Into this place called *sheol*, the soul of Jonah, as we shall see in our coming messages, descended for three days and three nights, while his body died in the belly of the whale. But as a perfect type of the Lord Jesus Christ, it was not digested nor corrupted. This was all in fulfillment of the prophecy concerning our Lord Jesus Christ in Psalm 16:

> For thou wilt not leave my soul in *sheol*; neither wilt thou suffer thine Holy One to see corruption (Ps. 16:10).

These words spoken by the prophet David, were a prophecy of the Death and Resurrection of the Lord Jesus Christ, and are quoted in the New Testament as referring to Him. And so, just as Jonah died and his body was entombed in the belly of the fish, while his soul went into *sheol*, so too, we shall see, when Jesus died, His spirit went back to the Father, His soul went down into *sheol*, while His body rested for three days and three nights in the tomb. This is the story of the Gospel. This is the story of God's plan of salvation for lost men and lost women. This was undoubtedly part of the message which Jonah conveyed to the Ninevites, and resulted in their repentance, and ultimate salvation. This is the Gospel in Jonah.

Chapter Eleven

WHERE ARE THE DEAD?

Out of the belly of hell cried I, and thou heardest my voice (Jonah 2:2).

THESE words were spoken by the prophet Jonah after he died in the belly of the fish. The word "hell," we have pointed out, in this verse is a mistranslation of the word, *sheol* in the original. Untold confusion has resulted from the failure of the translators to distinguish between *sheol*, and the grave, and hell. The word "hell" never occurs once in the Old Testament original. Wherever it occurs, it is a mistranslation of the word, *sheol*. The word "hell" in the New Testament is a translation of the word *gehenna*. It is used just eleven times in the Bible, and ten times it is used by Jesus, and only once in the epistle of James. In every case where it occurs in the original, it always refers to the place of the abode of the lost. There is no one in hell today. The first occupants will be the "beast and false prophets," who will be cast into this Lake of Fire at the beginning of the one thousand years of the millennium (Rev. 19:20). Then after the thousand years have been expired, the Devil himself, and his followers will be cast into the Lake of Fire to be tormented day and night forever and ever (Rev. 20:10).

SHEOL — NOT HELL

We have digressed here to make it clear that *sheol* and hell are not the same place. The wicked dead today are in *sheol*, and will not be cast into the Lake of Fire until the last judgment of the Great White Throne (Rev. 20:11-15).

Before Calvary, and the Resurrection of the Lord Jesus Christ, everyone who died, both saved and lost, went into this place called *sheol* in the Old Testament and *hades* in the New Testament. Consequently Jonah, when he died, went to this place.

We have already pointed out that the clearest description of this place is given by our Lord Himself in the actual account of the rich man and Lazarus in Luke 16. We would like to turn to it again. We have already seen the description of the place of the lost. The rich man was conscious, he remembered his past life, and moreover, we found it was a place of torment, from which there was no escape.

THE SAVED DIVISION

But now we come to the striking contrast in the condition of the saved, as represented by Lazarus. He was carried in safety to *sheol,* to the place called "Abraham's bosom." It is a picture of peace and rest. The bosom suggests safety, contentment and peace. It suggests the picture of a babe, snuggling at its mother's breast. The saved, therefore, who died and went to *sheol,* were in a place of wonderful peace.

Notice that Lazarus went to the same place as the rich man, *sheol,* but into the "saved" division of *hades.* He too was conscious and saw the rich man on the other side of the gulf. The question is often times asked, "Will there be recognition of our loved ones after death?" However, this is a question which, while it is asked again and again, should be settled by this passage alone, if there were nothing else in the Word of God. Will we remember and know each other in heaven? Certainly the rich man knew and remembered Lazarus in *sheol,* and called him by his name. Even the lost, therefore, in *hades,* will recognize those whom they knew here on earth. How much more, therefore, we who have been saved, and are bound for heaven!

Not only was Lazarus conscious after death, but he was in a place of comfort, for Jesus plainly says:

Lazarus . . . is comforted, and thou art tormented (Luke 16:25).

Then notice that it was a place of safety and security as well. This is guaranteed by the transportation which God provided for Lazarus upon his death. He was carried by angels into the place called "Abraham's bosom." He did not cross Jordan alone, but escorted by a heavenly host, he made his triumphal entry. How perfectly wonderful, when we come to the end of the road, that God will provide a heavenly escort to lead our triumphant journey into our Father's house. Then, too, we notice that it is a place of reunion, for he was taken into Abraham's bosom. The decease of the saints of the Old Testament is significantly described as being "gathered unto his fathers," or "his peoples." Abraham's bosom, therefore, suggests a place of reunion for those who in faith were the seed of Abraham. To this place Lazarus went at his death.

But now someone will immediately ask, "If *sheol* is in the heart of the earth, and a place of fire and brimstone, how can the saved who went there before Christ delivered them at His Resurrection, be happy and content in a place of flame and burning?" Ah, my friend, God is omnipotent, and He who could keep three Hebrew youths in a fiery furnace, heated seven times, so that they were neither hurt nor destroyed, is able to keep His own. Of the three Hebrews in the fiery furnace, we are told that not even the smell of fire clung to them. He was able to keep Daniel in the lion's den, and He certainly is able to keep His own, no matter what the conditions or circumstances may be.

THE GREAT DELIVERANCE

Now all we have said so far concerning *sheol* and *hades* as the place of the abode of the dead refers, of course, only to Old Testament saints who had died before the coming of the Redeemer. At Calvary and the Resurrection a great change took place in *sheol*, for when Jesus died His body was placed in a new tomb, but His soul descended into *sheol,* the place of the souls of the departed.

Before, however, taking up this important revelation, we want to answer one question, "Why did the souls of the saved under the Old Testament have to go into *sheol,* rather than going directly into the presence of God in heaven?" The believer who dies today since Calvary goes directly to heaven. Why then were not the Old Testament saints also immediately admitted into the presence of God? The answer lies in the nature of God, and the fact of sin. God is so perfectly holy, so righteous, and sin is so terrible and repugnant and awful in the sight of God, that He could not permit anyone with unatoned sin to come into His holy presence. Until the blood of Christ was shed, there could be no absolute payment for sin, no putting away of sin in the full sense of the word. God truly forgave sin before Calvary in the sense that He pardoned the Old Testament saints, but sin was never actually "put away" until Jesus said, "It is finished." The blood of bulls and goats and lambs and pigeons and the sacrifices of the Old Testament could not take away sin. And so God overlooked and pardoned and passed by the sins of the saints in the Old Testament, on the basis of the promise of a coming Redeemer, who by His own blood would "put away sin forever." God, therefore, saved the believer of the Old Testament, not on the basis of the blood of animal sacrifices, but in anticipation of the blood of Christ to which all of these pointed. But until that blood of Christ was literally shed, sin was never fully put away, but merely pardoned. On the promissory note, therefore, of Jesus that He would in the fulness of time pay the full debt for sin, God accepted the believer in the Old Testament, but the debt was not actually paid until Calvary. For this reason, an infinitely holy God could not allow anyone with fully unatoned sin in His presence, and so He provided for them a temporary abode in *sheol-hades,* from the time of their death until the Resurrection of Christ and their deliverance from the place of the dead.

THE GREAT CHANGE

At the time of Jesus' death, therefore, at Calvary, the saved were still in this place called *hades*. When the dying thief on the Cross confessed Jesus as Saviour, our Lord said to him, "today shalt thou be with me in paradise." Now notice that Jesus did not say, "Today shalt thou be with me in heaven," but instead, "paradise." Now, where was paradise at the time Jesus spoke those words? It was in the place where Jesus went on the day of His death. This is perfectly evident, for He said definitely, "Today shalt thou be with me in paradise."

But we also know that Christ went NOT into heaven on the day of His death, but into *sheol-hades*, for David says in Psalm 16:

> For thou wilt not leave my soul in *sheol*; neither wilt thou suffer thine Holy One to see corruption (Ps. 16:10).

And we know definitely from Peter's words on the day of Pentecost that these words refer to the Lord Jesus Christ. Peter in quoting Psalm 16 says:

> Therefore being a prophet, and knowing that God had sworn with an oath to him, that of the fruit of his loins, according to the flesh, he would raise up Christ to sit on his throne;
> He seeing this before spake of the resurrection of Christ, that his (Christ's) soul was not left in *sheol* (Acts 2:30, 31).

According to these words, therefore, the soul of Christ descended into *sheol-hades*, but came back from this place at His Resurrection. Since Jesus said to the dying thief, "Today shalt thou be with me in paradise," and on that day Jesus descended into *sheol*, we can be certain that paradise corresponds to the saved division of *sheol* in the heart of the earth.

WHY GO TO SHEOL?

But why did the soul of Jesus go to *sheol* at His death? The answer is clear when we remember that all the Old Testament saints were in this place until a full reconciliation could be made for their sins. When Jesus, therefore, cried,

"It is finished," the full payment for sin had been finally made, sin had been "put away," and He immediately went into *sheol* to proclaim the good news, and deliver them from their temporary confinement, and lead them triumphantly into heaven. Sin had been put away, and now the saints in Abraham's bosom could be released from *sheol*, and enter into the presence of God. This is the incident which Peter tells about in I Peter,

> For Christ also hath once suffered for sins, the just for the unjust, that he might bring us to God, being put to death in the flesh, but quickened by the Spirit:
> By which also he went and preached unto the spirits in prison;
> Which sometime were disobedient, when once the long-suffering of God waited in the days of Noah, while the ark was a preparing, wherein few, that is, eight souls were saved by water (I Pet. 3:18-20).

Here then we are told that Christ did go and preach unto the spirits which were in prison. These were in *sheol-hades*, and Paul refers to the same event when he says in Ephesians,

> Wherefore he saith, When he ascended up on high, he led captivity captive, and gave gifts unto men.
> Now that he ascended, what is it but that he also descended first into the lower parts of the earth?
> He that descended is the same also that ascended up far above all heavens, that he might fill all things (Eph. 4:8-10).

WHEN DID IT HAPPEN

After Jesus' Resurrection He brought these captives in *hades* out of the place of their temporary abode, into the permanent presence of God, for the work of redemption was now completed.

And so after Jesus' Resurrection, the saved division of *sheol-hades* was completely emptied. Remember the lost are still there. No change occurred in the lost division of *hades* at the Death and Resurrection of Christ. The lost will remain there until the judgment of the Great White Throne at the end of the ages, but the saints are now already in heaven. Today, therefore, since the Resurrection, the believer does not have to go into *hades* at all upon death, but goes directly into the presence of God. Paul the Apostle was able to say, "To be absent from the body is to be present with the Lord." David, the Old Testament saint, however, could never have said that. The most that David could ever say was, "Thou wilt not LEAVE my soul in *sheol*." He could not say with Paul, "To be absent from the body is to be present with the Lord."

In II Corinthians, chapter 12, Paul tells us that he had been caught up into paradise. Now we remind you again that when Jesus hung upon the Cross, paradise was still in *hades*, in the heart of the earth, for He said to the thief, "Today shalt thou be with me in paradise." But when Paul wrote II Corinthians, some thirty years after the Resurrection of Christ, he was caught up to the third heaven and into paradise. Sometime, therefore, between the Resurrection of Christ, and II Corinthians 12, paradise, the saved division of *hades* of the Old Testament, had been moved. Jesus went at His death to paradise to bring the glad news of full redemption and deliver the saints into the presence of God.

Today when the sinner dies, he still goes to *hades*. Finally, sinners will arise at the judgment of the Great White Throne in Revelation 20, and then, only then will they be cast into hell, also called the Lake of Fire.

And now in closing, we sum up the Bible teaching. Up until the Resurrection of Christ all who died went into *hades*; the lost in conscious suffering, and the saved in conscious bliss and comfort. When Jesus died He went down into *sheol*, and delivered the saved at His Resurrection, and took them to heaven where they await the first Resurrection. Not a single member of the Body of Christ, the Church of the New Testament, has ever gone or will ever have to go to *hades*. And this is undoubtedly what Jesus referred to when

He said, "The gates of *hades* (not hell) shall not prevail against it." It simply means that no member of the body of Christ will ever go to *hades*. And so we ask you in closing, to which class do you belong? There are only two possibilities. As we come to the end of this message we want to impress this fact upon you. If you are still unsaved, then your body will be buried when you die, your soul will go to the place of doom, and then at the last Resurrection, your unredeemed body will be raised and joined to your unredeemed soul, and together cast into the Lake of Fire. But if you are saved, then when you die your body will fall asleep, your soul will be escorted by a cohort of resplendent angels into the presence of God, and then when Jesus comes again, your body will awake, and be reunited with your soul, and you will spend eternity in His presence where sin and suffering and sorrow shall be no more. This is what John says in Revelation 21:

> And God shall wipe away all tears from their eyes; and there shall be no more death, neither sorrow, nor crying, neither shall there be any more pain: for the former things are passed away (Rev. 21:4).

To which class, my friend, do you belong? You can settle that issue right this moment before another minute passes, by turning in faith to the Lord Jesus Christ who died and rose for you, and receiving Him, believing His promise that,

> Him that cometh to me I will in no wise cast out (John 6:37).

Chapter Twelve

PARADISE — THEN AND NOW

> Now the Lord had prepared a great fish to swallow up Jonah. And Jonah was in the belly of the fish three days and three nights (Jonah 1:17).
> For as Jonah was three days and three nights in the whale's belly; so shall the Son of man be three days and three nights in the heart of the earth (Matt. 12:40).

THE sojourn of Jonah in the belly of the great fish is, as we have stated many times before, a picture of the Death of our Lord Jesus Christ, His burial and Resurrection. It is, therefore, not accidental that there are so many points of similarity in the record of Jonah and in the record of the Lord Jesus Christ.

SPECIALLY PREPARED PLACE

Notice first of all that Jonah and Christ were both buried in a specially prepared place, for the record reads:

> Now the Lord had prepared a great fish to swallow up Jonah (Jonah 1:17).

It was prepared beforehand for this special occasion, and just so, when our Lord died, God had a specially prepared place for His body, while His soul went into *sheol*. God had already prepared that place before the Lord's death that it might be ready for Him when He died. It was a new tomb in a garden "where never yet man had lain." Jonah's prepared place also was brand new. No one ever before had lain in the belly of a fish and survived. So too, the tomb in the garden

96

was a new tomb in which "never man had lain" before. Isaiah speaking in the fifty-third chapter tells us how far ahead the Lord had provided this place, for he says:

And he made his grave with the wicked, and with the rich in his death (Isa. 53:9).

In wealthy Joseph of Arimathaea's tomb they laid our Lord, and there His body rested for three days and three nights.

But while the body of Jonah slept in his strange tomb, his soul went down into *sheol*. The prayer in Jonah, chapter 2 was uttered while in the place of the departed souls of men. In the same way, while the body of Jesus rested in the tomb, His soul also went into *hades* in order to preach deliverance and bring the good news to the captives, and at His Resurrection lead them triumphantly into heaven.

WHERE IS SHEOL-HADES?

We come now to the interesting and important question, Where is *sheol-hades* located? Where is this place to which the soul of Jonah descended, and also where the soul of the Lord Jesus Christ went at His death? In Ephesians 4 we read:

Wherefore he saith, When he ascended up on high, he led captivity captive, and gave gifts unto men.

(Now that he ascended, what is it but that he also descended first into the lower parts of the earth?

He that descended is the same also that ascended up far above all heavens, that he might fill all things) (Eph. 4:8-10).

In this passage we are definitely told that the Lord Jesus Christ when He ascended, came up from the lower parts of the earth. This is definitely stated:

He that descended is the same also that ascended up far above all heavens, that he might fill all things (Eph. 4:10).

In the Book of Jonah, chapter 2 and verse 2, he cries out from the "belly of *sheol*." In verse 4 he is quoted as saying that he was cast out of God's sight. In verse 5 he confesses that the waters compassed him about "even to the soul." Then in verse 6 he tells us,

> I went down to the bottoms (roots) of the mountains, the earth with her bars was about me forever.

Notice carefully that he does not say that the waters were about him, but "the earth with her bars" was about him. He was, therefore, in the heart of the earth, where the mountains are rooted. In the same verse, he tells us that he was dead and resurrected, for he says:

> Yet hast thou brought up my life from corruption (Jonah 2:6).

He confesses that God raised him, that is, "brought up (his) life from corruption." It does not state that he was kept alive, but rather, brought back from death unto life.

HEART OF THE EARTH

Jesus said that as Jonah was, so would He be, in the heart of the earth. The tomb where His body was placed was, of course, not the heart of the earth. It was a sepulchre upon the surface of the earth. All of this leads us to ask again, "Does the Bible tell us exactly where this place, *sheol-hades*, is located?"

Jonah locates it at the bottoms of the mountains. Paul in Ephesians 4 describes Jesus as decending into the "lower parts of the earth." Our Lord also in Matthew 12:40 calls it "the heart of the earth." From these and other passages we can conclude that *sheol-hades*, (the place where the soul of Jonah, and the soul of the Lord Jesus Christ, together with all those who died before the Resurrection of Christ went), is somewhere in the heart of the earth. We would like to call your attention to one outstanding portion of Scripture which casts a great deal of light on this little-known and little-understood subject. It is found in Numbers 16. You may recall that Korah, Dathan and Abiram, who were among the children of Israel who left Egypt, fell to murmuring against Moses and Aaron in the wilderness, and despised God's appointed priesthood, and desired the office of priest, contrary to the command of God. As a result, God's anger arose against them, and we read this startling record in Numbers 16:

> And it came to pass, as he (Moses) had made an end of speaking all these words, that the GROUND clave asunder that was under them:
>
> And the EARTH opened her mouth, and swallowed them up, and their houses, and all the men that appertained unto Korah, and all their goods.
>
> They, and all that appertained to them, went DOWN ALIVE into the PIT, and the earth closed upon them: and they perished from among the congregation.
>
> And all Israel that were round about them fled at the cry of them: for they said, Lest the earth swallow us up also.
>
> And there came out a fire from the Lord, and consumed the two hundred and fifty men that offered incense (Num. 16: 31-35).

Now there are many things here which will make clear the teaching of the Word concerning *sheol* or *hades*, but first let me remind you that the word, "pit" in which Korah was swallowed up is SHEOL in the original. It is the same word used elsewhere for the place where the dead go, and is the Hebrew equivalent of the word, *hades*, used by the Lord Jesus in the story of the rich man and Lazarus. It is the same word used for the place from whence Jonah prayed and where Jesus went at His death, and "preached unto the spirits that were in prison," and from which He ascended when "He led captivity captive." So the passage should be read as follows, "they went down alive into *sheol*."

IN THE EARTH

Sheol then was in the heart of the earth. Upon the word of the Lord, the earth split open underneath these rebels. Whether it was by an earthquake or a miniature volcano makes no difference, the record says the "earth opened her mouth," and the rebels of Korah plunged into *sheol* through the fissure God created underneath them. There is no mis-

taking these words. They cannot be argued away or spirit-
ualized, for if you spiritualize SHEOL and the FIRE, then you
must do the same to the sons of Korah and their houses and
their rebellion, and we have nothing left. This is a historical
record given by God of the judgment of these men. Before
the earth closes upon these men who had rebelled against God,
we catch just a little glimpse of what there is below in the
place called *sheol*. We read that a "fire came out from the
Lord." The Lord sent the fire, but it came out of *sheol*
through the fissure in the earth. Do you doubt this? Do you
think that this was not LITERAL FIRE? Then listen. That
very same thing has happened a thousand times since, and
no one doubts that it is literal fire. I am referring now to
volcanic eruptions. Since the earth burst open in the days of
Korah and belched forth fire, this thing has been repeated
times without number. Again and again mountains have blown
up, and fire has shot forth from the bowels of the earth
thousands of feet into the air while the earth quaked, and
rivers of red hot lava poured down the mountain side. No
one doubts the reality of such incidents when they are re-
ported in the newspapers. No one doubts the literalness of
the fires which belch forth from volcanoes. We know of entire
cities being inundated and destroyed by molten flowing lava
and ash, and thousands of people perishing in the literal fires
which are spewed forth from the bowels of the mountains and
the heart of the earth. But when God says in His Word that
the earth opened her mouth and shot forth fire, and swallowed
up a few hundred men and houses, then men lift their eye-
brows in doubt, and reject it as fantastic, and make light of the
divine record, and insinuate that those who believe it are sim-
pletons and fools. We are told that we have long outgrown
belief in these antiquated, fossilized accounts of an outmoded
book, but recent discoveries of science have only corroborated
all that is written in the Bible.

ONLY TEMPORARY

This temporary abode of the lost is, therefore, definitely located in the center of the earth. When the earth shall be destroyed by fire at the end of time, *sheol-hades* will be transferred to the Lake of Fire as the permanent abode of the lost. Hell, therefore, today is empty, but John the revelator tells us plainly in Revelation that it will be the eternal abode of the Devil and his followers. In Revelation 20 we read:

> And I saw a great white throne, and him that sat on it, from whose face the earth and the heaven fled away; and there was found no place for them.
>
> And I saw the dead, small and great, stand before God; and the books were opened: and another book was opened, which is the book of life: and the dead were judged out of those things which were written in the books, according to their works.
>
> And the sea gave up the dead which were in it; and death and *hades* delivered up the dead which were in them: and they were judged every man according to their work (Rev. 20:11-13).

Here then we have the statement that at the end of time death and *hades* will be cast into the Lake of Fire. This, therefore, will follow the resurrection of the unjust, and eternity will set in.

And so we see that there is a future judgment and a future place of punishment for the wicked. The Bible clearly teaches all this. The awfulness of the judgment of God upon sin may be seen in the price which God demanded for our salvation. Nothing less than the infinite suffering and death of the Son of God Himself could atone for our sin. If, therefore, there is no future judgment of the sinner, then why did Christ have to die such an awful death? Then what did He come to save us from? Then Calvary becomes a mistake and an unnecessary blunder, and the Bible a book of sadistic superstition. If there is no hell and place of eternal punishment, then every gospel preacher who warns sinners to flee from the wrath to come is a despicable, repulsive, calamity howler, scaring people with non-existent consequences upon sin.

But if the Bible is true, and there is a Lake of Fire waiting for the lost, as the Bible clearly states, then the preacher, called to proclaim the whole counsel of God, who does not cry out with all his might to warn people of this place is untrue to his trust, and responsible for the souls of men. And so we shall never cease to cry out to men and women to flee to the Saviour, and escape from the wrath to come before it is forever too late. Jesus said in Luke 12:

> And I say unto you my friends, Be not afraid of them that kill the body, and after that have no more that they can do.
>
> But I will forewarn you whom ye shall fear: Fear him, which after he hath killed hath power to cast into hell; yea, I say unto you, Fear him (Luke 12:4, 5).

Oh, my friend, either these words of our Lord Jesus Christ are true or they are not true at all. It is one or the other. It cannot be anything else. If they are not true, then of course the Lord Jesus was mistaken, and we might just as well throw our entire Bible away. But these words *are* the truth, they are God's Word. It is what Jesus Himself said, and this being so, what else can I do as the messenger of God than cry out, "Hurry, hurry, hurry, flee from the wrath to come, before it is too late." I have no other alternative, as the words of Ezekiel ring again in my heart:

> When I say unto the wicked, Thou shalt surely die; and thou givest him not warning, nor speakest to warn the wicked from his wicked way, to save his life; the same wicked man shall die in his iniquity; but his blood will I require at thine hand (Ezek. 3:18).

Oh, may God help us to keep our hands clean of the blood of our fellow men. In our coming messages, the Lord willing, we shall speak on the location of hell, what it is, how long it will last, and other matters clearly revealed in the Bible. But before we close this message, I must tell you how you may escape this awful fate in the Lake of Fire.

God says He is not willing that any should perish, and He has made a way of escape through His Son, Jesus Christ, the Son of God, who died on the Cross and rose again from the grave to save you from eternal doom. His Word clearly says:

> He that heareth my word, and believeth on him that sent me, hath everlasting life, and shall not come into condemnation; but is passed from death unto life (John 5:24).
>
> For whosoever shall call upon the name of the Lord shall be saved (Rom. 10:13).

Oh, call on Him now. Cry to Him in faith to save you. Receive Him now, and believe His Word:

> Him that cometh to me I will in no wise cast out (John 6:37).

Chapter Thirteen

WHERE, WHAT, AND WHY IS HELL?

WE digress in our series on the Book of Jonah to consider the Bible teaching concerning the destiny of the lost in the Lake of Fire. Because of the teaching in the Book of Jonah concerning his descent into *sheol*, we feel that it will be helpful for a complete understanding of this subject concerning the place of the dead, to spend one message in discussing the Bible revelation concerning the Lake of Fire. What does the Bible teach about hell? The English word "hell" occurs some fifty-three times in our King James Version of the Scriptures; thirty-two times in the Old Testament, and twenty-one times in the New Testament. However, the word rendered "hell" in our English Bible is a translation of at least three different Hebrew words. The word "hell," when it occurs in the Old Testament should have been *sheol,* and never refers to "hell" at all, but instead to the temporary abode of the souls of the dead in the center of the earth, until the Resurrection of Jesus. Of the twenty-one times the word "hell" occurs in our King James Version of the New Testament, it is the translation of the word *hades* at least ten times.

In ten instances of the twenty-one occurrences of the word "hell" in the New Testament, it means NOT the eternal abode of the lost, or the Lake of Fire, but the temporary abode of the wicked in *sheol-hades,* until they will finally be cast into the Lake of Fire at the end of the ages (Rev. 20:14). In the balance of the instances where the word, "hell," occurs, it is a translation of quite another word, the Greek word *gehenna.*

And now here comes one of the most amazing, arresting things of all. In ten out of these eleven times where the word, *gehenna* occurs in the New Testament, it falls from the lips of the gentle Jesus, and is only once mentioned by any other (Jas. 3:6). I emphasize this tremendous fact — ten of the eleven occurrences in which the word, *gehenna* (hell) is used in the Bible, it is uttered by the loving, gentle, compassionate, kind and sympathetic Jesus who came to save people from hell. Twice it is used by Christ in His Sermon on the Mount. Again we emphasize this fact, because modern theology would do away with the fact of a literal hell. We are told over and over again that God is so loving, so kind, so long-suffering, so tender, that He would never even think of sending His creatures into a literal hell. We are told, therefore, not to preach on judgment and sin and condemnation and the Lake of Fire, for this is a medieval, outmoded doctrine, a hangover from the dark ages, and pagan polytheism. We are told instead to "preach the beatitudes, preach the Golden Rule, preach the Sermon on the Mount." Yes, indeed, we should preach the Sermon on the Mount, but if we do, we will have to preach on the subject of hell, for Jesus teaches clearly the doctrine of hell in this section of the Gospels (Matt. 5:22, 29).

A radio listener wrote some time ago, "No modern scholar believes in a hell anymore." Then I am not a scholar. But suppose that no intelligent scholar believes anymore in eternal punishment. What does that prove? It still does not change God's Word one iota. Of course, it just is not true that all scholarship has discarded belief in a literal hell. There are still thousands of the most scholarly men in the world who do believe it, and have been saved from it through faith in the Lord Jesus Christ.

I do not suppose there was a single scholar in Noah's day who believed a word that Noah was preaching concerning the coming flood, but it came just the same. There were no scholars in Lot's day who believed the coming judgment of

Sodom and Gomorrah, but it came just the same, and they perished in it. The scholars of Jesus' day paid but scant attention to our Lord when He warned of the destruction of Jerusalem and the judgment of God upon the nation of Israel, but it came just the same. Ah, yes, my friend, "Let God be true and every man a liar." Satan surely delivered a master stroke when he convinced man that hell was not real, but just a figment of the imagination, and an outmoded fancy. Few there are, therefore, who today still believe in a Bible hell. Men use the word so glibly, whereas if they only realized what the Bible says about it, they would tremble at the word. Today we hear on every hand and read in our magazines all sorts of joking about this awful place, and it is made the butt of many a gag and a joke to entertain the poor, blind souls who themselves face this awful doom.

BIBLE IS CLEAR

But the Bible teaches in no uncertain language the fact of a hell. Let me quote for you just a few passages taken verbatim from God's own Holy Word. In II Thessalonians Paul is speaking under inspiration concerning the Lord's coming, and says He will come,

> In flaming fire taking vengeance on them that know not God, and that obey not the gospel of our Lord Jesus Christ:
>
> Who shall be punished with everlasting destruction from the presence of the Lord, and from the glory of his power (II Thess. 1:8, 9).

And the Apostle John in Revelation tells us:

> But the fearful, and unbelieving, and the abominable, and murderers, and whoremongers, and sorcerers, and idolaters, and all liars, shall have their part in the lake which burneth with fire and brimstone: which is the second death (Rev. 21:8).

Or listen to the Lord Jesus Christ Himself as He describes the destiny of the wicked in Matthew 25:

> Then shall he say also unto them on the left hand, Depart

from me, ye cursed, into everlasting fire, prepared for the devil and his angels;

And these shall go away into everlasting punishment: but the righteous into life eternal (Matt. 25:41, 46).

It is hardly necessary, I am sure, to quote additional passages to show what the Bible says about the future destiny of the wicked.

MUST BE HELL

But wholly apart from the Bible, hell is a moral necessity in our universe. Do away with the punishment of evildoers, and the whole moral fabric and integrity of society breaks down completely. The basis of all good government is justice. Evildoers must be punished. We have laws to punish the thief, the murderer, the liar, the robber, the traitor, the rebel. No one denies that this is just and right. Every jail and prison in the world is a monument to the necessity of a moral government and the justice of punishing the criminal. What a world this would be if there were no laws to govern, and no penalty for the criminal who commits a crime against human authority. No one objects to this. But when God Who is the Supreme Ruler of the universe, insists upon punishing evil, then people put up a great howl of an unjust and an arbitrary God, and call Him a cruel monster.

In addition to all this, unless there is a place of future punishment, then the Cross of Christ and the sacrifice of our Saviour become a divine blunder. When we look at Calvary, and see the terrific and terrible price that God demanded of His own Son, after He became sin for us, and was willing to die in our place, we cannot but realize the awful doom from which He came to save us. Calvary stands, therefore, as the great argument to the holiness of God, and the moral necessity of a hell. The background of Calvary is judgment and God's hatred for sin, and if the Lord Jesus Christ had to pay that infinite price for sin to save us, then we can only imagine what the doom of the lost must be.

Did God Create Hell?

When God created the heavens and the earth, He did not include a place of punishment for the wicked. Just when God created the place called the Lake of Fire and "hell" in the Scriptures, we do not know. In the plan of God's original creation described in Genesis, "hell" was not included. That must have been a subsequent provision. In Genesis 1:1 we read:

In the beginning God created the heaven and the earth.

The record mentions the heaven and the earth, but strange as it may seem, there is no mention of a hell. The Bible does not say, "In the beginning God created the heaven and the earth and hell." Hell is significantly omitted. Of course, God being omniscient knew that sin would come, and a hell would become necessary later on, but before sin entered, there was no hell prepared by God. Hell was a later provision.

When Was It Prepared?

The question then arises, "When did God prepare this Lake of Fire?" To this we cannot give a positive, definite answer, but it must have been after the fall of the angels. From the Book of Job we learn that the angels (called "morning stars") were present at the original creation of the earth. There is much evidence that the original earth, millions upon millions of years ago, was the habitation of these created angels. And then Lucifer, the archangel, and the leader of the angelic hosts, rebelled against Almighty God with a host of lesser angelic beings, and as a result was cast both out of the earth, and out of heaven, and banished to the upper atmosphere.

Now because of the sin of these fallen angels, God prepared a place to which they will be consigned in everlasting damnation, to be tormented day and night forever and ever (Rev. 20:10). This is plain from a statement of our blessed Lord Himself in Matthew 25:41,

> Then shall he say also unto them on the left hand, Depart from me, ye cursed, into everlasting fire, PREPARED FOR THE DEVIL AND HIS ANGELS.

What a tremendously solemn revelation! The fires of everlasting hell were never meant for mankind. They were never meant for you, my poor sinner friend. They were prepared for the Devil and his angels. God never made man for hell, nor did He make hell for man. If man goes there, it will be only because he chooses to do so by refusing to receive God's wonderful gift of love and salvation. You will never be able to blame God for sending you into the everlasting fires.

Only Two Masters

There are only two masters, Christ and the Devil. And you, my friend, as well as I, can only serve one of these. It must be one or the other. Jesus said: "No man can serve two masters." And if you serve Christ here below, it is wholly just and fitting and right that you should spend eternity in bliss in heaven with the One whom you loved and served here below.

But if you choose to serve the Devil, and refuse to receive the Lord Jesus Christ, it is only right and just and proper that you should spend eternity with your master, whom you have chosen to serve.

Hell never was meant for you, and God does not want you to go there. If you do, it will be your own fault in refusing to receive God's offer of heaven and salvation. If you end up in the place of eternal doom, it will be over the very body of the Crucified Son of God.

Another question which arises is,

Where Is Hell?

"Where is the Lake of Fire?" Again the Bible gives no definite answer. It may be some blazing star a million light years removed from this earth. It may be some burned out ruined planet. We just don't know. One or two things we do know, however. It is complete separation from God, the God of light. He says, "Depart from me, ye wicked, into the place prepared for the devil and his angels." And it is called the "place of outer darkness." But the exact location is not revealed in Scripture.

DEGREES IN GEHENNA

Before we close this message, however, there is one more thing that we want to make clear. While hell is described in the Bible as a place of torment and suffering, not all the occupants in the Lake of Fire will, by any means, suffer in the same degree. To some, hell will be a little heaven compared with what it will be for others. God's judgment will be according to justice and righteousness, for "his mercy endureth forever." It will be absolutely fair and just.

Nowhere is this more clearly taught than in Revelation 20:

> And I saw a great white throne, and him that sat on it, from whose face the earth and the heaven fled away; and there was found no place for them.
> And I saw the dead, small and great, stand before God; and the books were opened: and another book was opened, which is the book of life: and the dead were judged out of those things which were written in the books, ACCORDING TO THEIR WORKS (Rev. 20:11, 12).

Now I would have you notice particularly those words, ACCORDING TO THEIR WORKS. This same thing is repeated again in verse 13. This judgment, therefore, is according to their works. It is to determine the DEGREE of their punishment. The destiny of the lost was settled forever when they died. That was determined by their rejection of the Lord Jesus Christ. Salvation does not depend upon works, but on faith alone. But here at the final judgment these lost ones whose eternal abode in hell was already determined and settled by their rejection of Christ, are now to be judged as to the degree of their punishment, determined by the light which they have rejected, the opportunities they have enjoyed, and the works which they have done.

It will be infinitely more tolerable in the day of judgment for the pagan who never heard the Gospel at all, than for you who have heard and rejected the invitation of the grace of God over and over again. I repeat, therefore, that hell will be a heaven for some who have never had the opportunities, and the light of the Gospel, compared to those of you who have lived in Christian lands, heard the Gospel over and over again, and then rejected it. And so we repeat, that not all will suffer alike in the Lake of Fire. It will depend upon the opportunity which has been rejected. If you are going to be lost, my friend, it would be infinitely better if you had never heard the message of salvation; yea, it would be better for you if you had never been born. The very fact that you have again once more heard the warning increases your responsibility, and leaves you without any excuse.

But there is no need for any of you to fear this awful judgment, for God has made full and adequate provision to save you. Hell is the place prepared for the Devil and his angels, but He has also prepared a place in heaven for all those who will trust Him and receive Jesus Christ as Lord and Saviour.

> For God so loved the world, that he gave his only begotten Son, that whosoever believeth in him should not perish, but have everlasting life (John 3:16).

Chapter Fourteen

THE GOOD FRIDAY MYTH

> And he began to teach them, that the Son of man must suffer many things, and be rejected of the elders, and of the chief priests, and scribes, and be killed, and AFTER THREE DAYS rise again (Mark 8:31).
>
> Saying, Sir, we remember that that deceiver said, while he was yet alive, AFTER THREE DAYS I will rise again (Matt. 27:63).
>
> And that he was buried, and that he rose again the THIRD DAY according to the scriptures (I Cor. 15:4).
>
> And Jonah was in the belly of the whale three days and three nights (Jonah 1:17).

OF all the people in the world who have lived and died, there is not another who had such an experience as the prophet Jonah. To be cast overboard in a storm as the only means of quieting the tempest and thus saving others imperiled by the storm which he had brought about, and then to be promptly swallowed by a great fish, to die in the fish's belly but not be digested or corrupted, and then to be raised again after three days to become the great preacher to the Gentiles, constitutes an experience the like of which has never before fallen to any other man. Yet, there the story stood on the inspired page of Scripture for over six hundred years before anyone knew the real meaning and purpose of the record. It was just the humanly incredible story of a Hebrew prophet.

Then Jesus came, and in one brief flash of illumination gave meaning and purpose to the entire exciting narrative. In a remarkably few words the Son of God in Matthew 12 illuminates the Book of Jonah with divine light, lifting it out of the realm of mere history or speculation, setting it totally aside from tradition, fable, fancy or fiction, and shows us its real meaning. It is a picture of the Death and the Resurrection of Christ Himself. It is the Gospel according to Jonah.

As we examine the history of Jonah we discover the Gospel. It is one of the fullest and clearest types of the mighty work of Jesus Christ in the entire realm of divine revelation. No great wonder, therefore, that the Devil has directed his special attack against the Book of Jonah. Men of corrupt minds, who have not the spirit of Christ though they call themselves by His Name, ridicule and doubt the narrative, and seek to show their superior wisdom and scholarship by casting aspersions upon the one book of Scripture which more than any other has set forth the sufferings of Christ and the glory that should follow.

On the one hand there are those who flatly deny the historicity of Jonah. Then there are others who seek to pull the story down to the level of natural law, and seek to prove that there was nothing miraculous or supernatural in Jonah's experience. They admit it was an unusual, but not necessarily a miraculous experience. They cite instances of fish swallowing men who survived a few hours, and then were taken out alive, unconscious, macerated and mauled, but still alive. And they say, "See! here is a case where a man survived a few hours in the belly of a fish, so therefore, we can believe the story of Jonah to be true." This is one of the most subtle forms of unbelief and infidelity, more dangerous than an outright denial of the story itself. They have never produced a single case of a man who was in the stomach of a fish seventy-two hours and came out alive and unharmed. When Jonah, after his sojourn in the fish for three days came forth, he was none the worse for his experience. He was not unconscious, he was not macerated and mauled, apparently showed no ill effects from his experience, but was able and ready to go immediately and carry out his divine commission. All of it was because, as a type of the Lord Jesus Christ, Jonah had died, but his body was supernaturally preserved from corruption. This David had already prophesied and foretold in Psalm 16, in speaking of the Lord Jesus Christ:

> Thou wilt not leave my soul in *sheol;* neither wilt thou suffer thine Holy One to see corruption (Ps. 16:10).

A THIRD ERROR

But there is a third subtle error which the enemy of our souls has foisted upon us in his attempt to discredit both Jonah the type, and the Lord Jesus Christ the antitype. It is by the subtle addition of religious tradition to the simple record of the Word of God. It is the unfounded tradition that Jesus was crucified on Good Friday (so-called) and arose at or slightly before sunrise on Sunday morning. And that tradition is held in the face of the repeated statement of Jesus and the apostles that He was in the grave three days and three nights, and would arise after three days and three nights. It is, however, asserted that the ancient rabbis counted part of a day as a whole day, and thus we have a couple of hours on Friday, all day Saturday, and a few hours on Sunday, and that is supposed to be three days and three nights. But our Lord Jesus Himself said "three days and three nights," and not one day and two nights.

ONE DAY IS CERTAIN

So we want to re-examine the record more carefully, that we may arrive at the truth. In seeking the truth, we call your attention to a number of facts:

The Jewish day began at sundown and ended at sundown. It was not from midnight to midnight as it is generally observed today. In the Bible the twenty-four hour day began in the evening, not at midnight. This rule was laid down back in the account of creation in Genesis 1. At the close of the first day of creation, we read:

And the evening and the morning were the first day (Gen. 1:5).

So it was with the other days as well (Gen. 1:8, 13, 19, 23).

This method of reckoning from sundown to sundown is still observed by the orthodox Jews in their feast days and sabbath days. The Jewish sabbath begins at sundown, or six o'clock on Friday, and closes on Saturday at sundown. So will you remember that the twenty-four hour day in Scriptures begins at sundown. Thus the first day of the week on which Jesus arose began not at midnight on Saturday but at six o'clock of our own Saturday evening. Evidently then, Jesus arose not at sun-up on the first day of the week, but immediately after sundown on our Saturday evening, which would be the first day of the week. This is evident from all of the records. Matthew says, for instance, in Matthew 28:1,

> In the end of the sabbath, as it began to dawn toward the first part of the week, came Mary Magdalene. . . .

Will you notice Mary visited the tomb at dawn, and at that time Jesus had already arisen from the tomb, for the tomb was found to be empty. Mark tells us the following about the visit of the two Marys:

> And very early in the morning the first day of the week, they came unto the sepulchre at the rising of the sun (Mark 16:2).

But again the tomb was already found empty, for Jesus had already arisen sometime previously. And Luke gives us this information:

> Now upon the first day of the week, very early in the morning, they came unto the sepulchre (Luke 24:1).

And again we find that the tomb was already empty. The apostle John adds in John 20:1,

> The first day of the week cometh Mary Magdalene early, when it was YET DARK (John 20:1).

Mary then came while it was yet dark, before sunrise, before the dawning of the day. How early she came we are not told, but it was still night, and Jesus was already gone. From these Scriptures, therefore, we learn that Jesus was not resurrected at sunrise, for in each case, even before dawn, the tomb was already empty. Jesus arose early on the first day, which would be at the beginning of the first day, on our Saturday night.

GOOD FRIDAY

Now if the Good Friday tradition, which is generally observed, is true, and it is a fact that part of a day counts as a whole day, then we still cannot crowd in three days between Friday night and Saturday afternoon. Since Jesus arose at the close of the seventh day right after sundown, it would still only make two days or part of two days, an hour or two on Friday (for He died at three o'clock in the afternoon) and Saturday. But the thing becomes still more absurd when we remind you that Jesus was actually in the tomb only one day, if the Friday Crucifixion is correct. Remember that Jesus died at three o'clock on the day of His Crucifixion. There were only three hours left of that day, from three to six, before the Sabbath would begin. At six o'clock, the sabbath legally began in the land of Palestine. There were then only three hours left into which to crowd all of the events which followed, and are recorded so meticulously in the Scriptures. First of all, will you notice that the soldiers pierced His side after three o'clock and the blood and the water poured forth, as proof that Jesus was dead. But even before this the Jews had requested that the bones of the victims be broken, and they be put to death, lest the sabbath should be defiled. This probably meant a trip to Jerusalem. John gives us the record in John 19:31-34. Remember that all of these things happened after three o'clock in the afternoon, and before six o'clock at night.

But that was not all. After all this had happened, we find that Joseph of Arimathaea also made a trip to the city of Jerusalem, and requested of Pilate that he might take the body of Jesus and bury it:

> And now when the even was come, because it was the preparation, that is, the day before the sabbath,
> Joseph of Arimathaea, an honourable counsellor, which also waited for the kingdom of God, came, and went in boldly unto Pilate, and craved the body of Jesus (Mark 15:42, 43).

This trip to Pilate must have consumed some considerable time. But there is even more. Joseph having received permission from Pilate, preparing to bury the body of the Lord Jesus after he had interviewed Pilate, had to do some shopping before the stores closed for the sabbath at six o'clock. And so we read in Mark 15:46:

> And he bought fine linen, and took him down, and wrapped him in the linen, and laid him in a sepulchre which was hewn out of a rock, and rolled a stone unto the door of the sepulchre.

Now having bought the linen and the spices, Joseph hurries out of the city to the Cross, takes down the body, assisted by Nicodemus, wraps it in the linen which he had purchased, and carries Him to the sepulchre. All of these things, we remind you, had to be done in the space of just three hours. The breaking of the bones of the thieves, the piercing of Jesus' side, the trip by Joseph to Pilate, his purchase of the fine linen, and then his return to Golgotha and taking the body from the Cross, wrapping it in the linen, and burying it in the tomb — all this in three hours' time. We wonder how it could be done. Certainly we may assume the body was not laid in the tomb until almost the deadline six o'clock. This being so, how can we possibly get in more than one day from Friday evening to Saturday evening? Actually it was only one night and one day — instead of three days and three nights, if the Friday Crucifixion is correct.

WHAT IS THE DIFFERENCE?

In our next message we shall thoroughly explode the Good Friday tradition from the Scriptures, and prove that Jesus was crucified on Wednesday, and not on Friday. But before we close this message, we want to answer one question which undoubtedly has arisen in the minds of many of you. You are probably tempted to ask, "Well, what is the difference after all? Is the question worth all of this discussion? Supposing Jesus was crucified on Wednesday, what harm is there in keeping it as Good Friday?"

To all of this we would answer that it is vitally important, for on it depends the truthfulness and authority of the Lord Jesus Christ. Remember while Jesus was here, His authority as the Son of God was challenged by the scribes and the Pharisees. They asked Him for evidence of His authority as the Son of God. Notice the Pharisees' question. They said

Master, we would see a sign from thee (Matt. 12:38).

They demanded some evidence, some proof, some sign of His authority. And it was to this challenge that Jesus replied in the now familiar words:

For as Jonas was three days and three nights in the whale's belly; so shall the Son of man be three days and three nights in the heart of the earth (Matt. 12:40).

Jesus, therefore, stakes His authority as the Son of God on being in the tomb for three days and three nights. If our Lord, therefore, was NOT buried three whole days and three whole nights, then He is not the infallible Son of God, then He must have been mistaken, and we cannot trust Him fully. He said, "three days and three nights." If it was not so, then how can we believe anything else which He has said.

Salvation is by believing the Word of God, just as God gave it and as God meant it. It is not in ceremonies of Lent and Good Friday and Easter, and all of the other attachments of religion. It is not in believing tradition, or observing holy days. It is personal faith in a personal Christ who died on the Cross, and after three days arose again. May we, therefore, believe God's Word upon the simple record, and not be misguided by the opinions and traditions of men. May we look away from pagan tradition, and trust the One who said,

> Come unto me, all ye that labour and are heavy laden, and I will give you rest (Matt. 11:28).

Chapter Fifteen

THE WEDNESDAY CRUCIFIXION

OUR Lord Jesus Christ was crucified on Wednesday, He died at three o'clock Wednesday afternoon, and was buried at or about sundown that same evening, and remained in the tomb until Saturday evening, and arose at the conclusion of the sabbath. The Jewish day began at sundown and ended at sundown. Hence, Jesus was in the tomb from Wednesday evening until Saturday evening, arising at the beginning of the first day of the week which began immediately after sundown. Only thus can we understand the words of our Lord Jesus, that like Jonah, He would be in the heart of the earth for "three days and three nights."

BIBLE DEFINITION

The Bible clearly defines for us the use of the words "day" and "night." Wherever the words are used to apply to a day of the week or month, they always indicate exactly what is meant. The word, DAY, is also used to express indefinite periods of time, such as "day of the Lord," "the day of vengeance," the "day of calamity," the "day of visitation," etc., but in these instances, the context always clearly indicates that it refers not to a literal day, but rather to a period of time. In every instance where a twenty-four hour day is referred to, the meaning is clear from the context, that it has reference to the light part and the dark part of that particular day. The Bible gives God's own definition of "day and night." In Genesis 1 we read:

> And God saw the light, that it was good: and God divided the light from the darkness.

> And God called the light Day, and the darkness he called
> Night. And the evening and the morning were the first day
> (Gen. 1:4, 5).

Here then is God's definition of day and night, constituting
one complete day. It consists of a light period and a dark
period, according to the clear teaching of this verse in Genesis.
Now if we apply this definition to Jesus' words, we would
read as follows: "As Jonah was three light periods and three
dark periods in the whale's belly, so also shall the Son of man
be three light periods and three dark periods in the heart of
the earth." With this interpretation our Lord Himself agrees.
In John 11:9 He says:

> Are there not twelve hours in the day? If any man walk in
> the day, he stumbleth not (John 11:9).

Here our Lord says that the day is twelve hours of light,
and hence, the night means twelve hours of darkness. Surely
the meaning of "three days and three nights" must become
clear from these indisputable passages of Scripture. Since the
Lord Jesus, therefore, rose early after sundown on the first day
of the week, we have but to reckon back three days (3 x 12)
and three nights (3 x 12) and we have seventy-two hours,
which brings us to Wednesday evening at sundown when He
was buried.

One more example of the meaning of "day and night" in
the Bible. In Exodus 13:21 we read:

> And the Lord went before them by DAY in a pillar of cloud
> . . . and by NIGHT in a pillar of fire . . . to go by day and
> night.

From this again it is seen that the use of the words, "day
and night," refers to the light and the dark periods of the
twenty-four hour day. There is, therefore, not a shred of Bible
evidence that we are to take part of a day as a complete
period of twenty-four hours consisting of a day and a night.
The assumption that a part of a day counts for a whole day
was taken from the Talmud, and is not found at all in the

Bible. The Friday Crucifixion, therefore, is a mere tradition, meekly accepted but totally without any foundation in the Bible.

WHENCE THE ERROR

We come, therefore, to a question, which is an important one. "Where then did this baseless tradition of Good Friday originate?" It all started with a misunderstanding of the statement, that the day following the Crucifixion was to be the sabbath. In Luke we read, concerning the day of Jesus' death:

> And that day was the preparation and the sabbath drew on (Luke 23:54).

The day after the Crucifixion was the sabbath. We have another similar passage recorded in Mark 15:42 where we read:

> And now when the even was come, because it was the preparation, that is, the day before the sabbath,
> Joseph of Arimathaea, an honourable counsellor, which also waited for the kingdom of God, came, and went boldly unto Pilate, and craved the body of Jesus.

Here then we have a clear statement that the day following the death and the burial of the Lord Jesus was the sabbath. But it does not state in this verse WHICH SABBATH it happened to be. It is not stated here or anywhere else that it was the weekly sabbath of the Decalogue which fell on Saturday of each week. We must not forget that Israel had many sabbath days in their ceremonial year. These are minutely described in Leviticus 23 which we suggest for your study. Seven of these sabbath days are mentioned in their order as follows:

1. The Passover Sabbath on the fourteenth day of the first month.

2. The Unleavened Bread Sabbath on the very next day, the fifteenth day of the first month.

3. The Feast of Firstfruits on the seventeenth day of the month.

4. The Feast of Pentecost, fifty days later.

5. The Feast of Trumpets, in the seventh month.

6. The Feast of Atonement.

7. The Feast of Tabernacles.

Every one of these days was a "sabbath" of rest, and they are so-called in the Bible. Each was a day of complete cessation of all labor, and therefore, a sabbath day (see Lev. 23:25).

Concerning the Feast of Trumpets, God said, for instance:

> It shall be unto you a sabbath of rest . . . in the ninth day of the month at even, from even to even, shall ye celebrate your sabbath (Lev. 23:32).

In Leviticus 23:39 we read concerning the Feast of Tabernacles:

> Also in the fifteenth day of the seventh month . . . ye shall keep a feast unto the Lord seven days: on the first day shall be a sabbath, and on the eighth day shall be a sabbath.

From these you will see that the "sabbath" did not always refer to the seventh day of the week by any means, but might fall on any other day. We have given in detail these facts because so many ignorantly imagine every time the word "sabbath" appears anywhere in the Bible it must always refer to the weekly, seventh-day sabbath. But this weekly sabbath was only one of many sabbaths. The sabbath following the Death and Burial of the Lord Jesus Christ was NOT the weekly sabbath at all as we shall see from other passages of Scripture. Failure to recognize this has led to the "Friday Crucifixion" delusion.

The Bible is crystal clear that this sabbath following the Crucifixion, was the Passover sabbath. In John 19 the Holy Spirit informs us concerning Christ's Crucifixion:

> And it was the preparation of the passover, and about the sixth hour: and he (Pilate) saith unto the Jews, Behold your King! (John 19:14)

Now here we have the definite statement that the day following the Crucifixion of Christ was the preparation of the

Passover sabbath. The next day was the Passover day. That there might be no doubt about this, John adds in verse 31:

> The Jews therefore, because it was the preparation, that the bodies should not remain upon the cross on the sabbath day, (for that sabbath day was an HIGH DAY,) besought Pilate that their legs might be broken, and that they might be taken away (John 19:31).

Will you notice the words in the parentheses which John inserts. It was a sabbath, to be sure, but not the ordinary weekly sabbath, and so he adds by way of explanation: "FOR THAT SABBATH DAY WAS AN HIGH DAY."

It is, therefore, sharply differentiated as an unusual sabbath, and not the common weekly sabbath. He seems to say, Don't confuse this sabbath with the weekly sabbath, for this was "an high day." The Passover sabbath was the greatest day in the calendar of Israel, and so is set aside by John to indicate which day followed the Crucifixion of Christ.

THREE SABBATHS

During the week in which Jesus was crucified, there were at least three sabbath days. On Thursday, the fourteenth of the month, was the Passover sabbath. Friday, the fifteenth, was the sabbath of unleavened bread. Saturday, the sixteenth of the month was the weekly sabbath, and all these three sabbath days Jesus spent in the tomb, in the place of death. This is further stated in Matthew 28:1,

> In the end of the sabbath, as it began to dawn toward the first day of the week, came Mary Magdalene and the other Mary.

The word translated "sabbath" in this verse is plural (*sabbaton*) and literally reads, "In the end of the sabbath days" (that is, at the end of the three successive sabbath days in that one week) Jesus arose. All of this, of course, has its message for us, and is by design of Almighty God. Had Jesus been crucified in any other year than the year in which He was crucified, these three sabbaths would not have occurred in that particular order. Jesus, therefore, spent three sabbath days in the tomb. Now we know that the sabbaths were a part of the law, whether it be a ceremonial sabbath, or the sabbath of the Ten Commandments. We also know that the law is the ministry of death. The law demanded the death penalty for the sinner. The law demanded perfection. It could not save the sinner; it could only put the sinner to death. And so the Lord Jesus came to take the sinner's place, and God "laid on Him the iniquity of us all," and the curse of the law, which is death, fell upon Him, and therefore, he spent three legal sabbath days in the place of death, fulfilling the law, satisfying its justice, and,

> Having abolished in his flesh the enmity, even the law of commandments contained in ordinances; for to make in himself of twain one new man, so making peace (Eph. 2:15).

In Colossians 2:14, 15 we are told that Christ blotted out,

> . . . the handwriting of ordinances that was against us, which was contrary to us, and took it out of the way, nailing it to his cross;
> And having spoiled principalities and powers, he made a shew of them openly, triumphing over them in it.

DEAD TO THE LAW

Yes, the Lord Jesus fulfilled all the demands of the law, not only the ceremonial sabbath days, but the sabbath of the decalogue as well. And then He arose at the end of the three sabbaths, and so today we are not saved by keeping sabbath days which have been abolished, but we are redeemed by personal faith in the finished work of the Lord Jesus Christ, and now serve Him out of a heart of love, and rejoice in the Resurrection of our precious Saviour. Paul says in Galatians 2:

> For I through the law am dead to the law, that I might live unto God (Gal. 2:19).

To seek salvation, therefore, through the works of the law is to remain under the sentence of death. To turn back again to the observance of the legal seventh day sabbath, is to deny the finished work of Christ, and so Paul admonishes us:

> Let no man therefore judge you in meat, or in drink, or in respect of an holyday, or of the new moon, or of the SABBATH DAYS:
>
> Which are a shadow of things to come; but the body is of Christ (Col. 2:16, 17).

We, today, have a living Saviour, one who conquered death. We are not saved by the law, but by the grace of God. How many there are today who have never learned to live by grace, but measure their fellowmen and their fellow Christians only by what they do or do not do on the so-called sabbath days. This was the tragic mistake of the ones who killed Christ. Listen to the record, for an example of bigoted sabbatarianism. John says that the accusers of Christ,

> . . . went not into the judgment hall, lest they should be defiled; but that they might eat the passover (John 18:28).

What hypocrisy! What legalistic blindness! They would not defile themselves on the preparation day, so they could observe their legal sabbath, but they could murder the Son of God on the day before the sabbath. They could murder Jesus the day before the sabbath, but His body must be taken from the Cross before the sabbath itself arrived, lest they themselves should be legally defiled. Oh, the utter blindness of those who are under the law, who know not the grace of God.

How many today are no better! All their religion is wrapped up in one day. Millions who know not that the sabbath is the symbol of death, have called the first day of the week the "Christian sabbath," and know not that we now live in Resurrection light, and we serve Him because we have been delivered from the curse of the law. They measure all their fellow men by the rod of their sabbath. All week long they can scheme and connive and cheat and live for self, but comes the sabbath, they must not be defiled. Comes the so-called sabbath and they pack away their trappings of the week, and put on their Sunday clothes, and by pious airs seek to cover up that which has been inconsistently practiced all week.

Beloved, every day should be the Lord's Day for the believer. Let us not come like the women weeping over a Christ whom they supposed was dead, but let us rejoice in One who is alive, and dedicate our lives seven days a week to His wonderful service.

Sinner, here is the lesson for you. There is no salvation by your religion, by your efforts, by your own works of the law, for Christ is the end of the law to everyone who believeth. You must come, and be willing to say:

> Not the labor of my hands,
> Could fulfil Thy law's demands;
> Could my zeal no respite know,
> Could my tears forever flow;
> These for sin could not atone,
> Thou must save, and Thou alone.

Chapter Sixteen

HOW LONG IS "THREE DAYS AND NIGHTS"?

> But I will sacrifice unto thee with the voice of thanksgiving;
> I will pay that that I have vowed. SALVATION IS OF THE LORD
> (Jonah 2:9).

SALVATION is of the Lord! These were the last five words
which Jonah spake before he was delivered from the belly
of the fish. And they were spoken from the strangest place
in the entire world. They were uttered by the soul of a
dead man in the inwards of a sea monster. It was a cry of
both hopelessness and despair, as well as triumphant hope.
Hopeless despair at his own failure to save himself — and a cry
of hope and victory in the ability of God to save.

But Jonah did not utter these final words until he had
come to the very end of himself. He had come to the end of
his rope, so to speak, and these words were the expression of
his complete submission to the will of God. Poor Jonah had
imagined that he could run away from the Lord, but God
had sent a mighty tempest to overtake him. But Jonah was
not yet convinced, and sought refuge in a sinking ship, and
fell fast asleep. He was cast into the sea, and was swallowed
by a fish, and it took three days for Jonah to come to himself
and confess that "salvation is of the Lord."

We must not imagine that Jonah was swallowed without
a struggle. We do not even know if Jonah could swim, but
we may rest assured that he did his best to get away from
the jaws of the fish, and knowing what a temperamental man
Jonah was, we can only imagine what trouble he must have
given the fish in getting him down. I am quite convinced that

Jonah squirmed and struggled, kicked and bit and scratched the throat of the fish all the way going down. And it is inconceivable that after he arrived in the belly of the fish, that even then he gave up without a struggle. He was, to be sure, in the place of death, and poor Jonah must have called upon all his tricks and ingenuity in his efforts to extricate himself before he died. He must have kicked and butted and scratched and bitten that poor fish in an effort to encourage it to disgorge this troublesome piece of bait. Maybe Jonah carried a knife, and tried to hack his way out. We don't know, of course, but whatever he did, it was of no avail until he gave up and cried out,

Salvation Is of the Lord!

And what a picture all of this presents of the sinner in the place of death. For Jonah is not only a picture of our Lord Jesus Christ, as we have seen, in the place of Death and Resurrection, but he is also a picture of the sinner whose place Jesus took. God's salvation in bringing the sinner out of spiritual death and the dominion and power of the enemy, and giving him new life in a new way, is illustrated in the story of Jonah. But God will not bring this deliverance until man has ceased from his own efforts and struggles to save himself. God's salvation is only for those who admit they are lost. So long as the sinner imagines that he can save himself, there is no hope for him. Just so long as he thinks he can raise a single little finger toward his own deliverance, God will not save him. He must be brought to the place where he will acknowledge that "salvation is of the Lord."

But Jonah did not make the mistake of modern theology today, which teaches that we do not even need His salvation. Jonah knew that he was lost, and tried his best to get out of his terrible condition. We are by nature in the place where Jonah found himself. We too have been swallowed up by a great monster. We too are in a world of tempest and storm and threatening doom. This world is headed for destruction, and we are sailors upon it. A radio commentator recently quoted a reliable diplomat as saying that Russia and the United States now have a sufficient stock pile of "A" bombs to blow up the entire earth. The Bible clearly states that someday this old world will be destroyed. Peter tells us in II Peter 3:10,

> But the day of the Lord will come as a thief in the night; in the which the heavens shall pass away with a great noise, and the elements shall melt with fervent heat, the earth also and the works that are therein shall be burned up.

This world, like the sea into which Jonah was cast, is a dangerous place to live in. But in addition to being cast into a troubled sea, we have also been swallowed up by that awful monster called sin, for John says:

> The whole world lieth in wickedness (I John 5:19b).

Like Jonah, the seed of Adam came into this place because of disobedience to God's Word. And like Jonah, they have no way of escape by themselves, even though men try to invent ways of minimizing their condition by all manner of self-discipline and improvement of their environment. Man is clever, and invents many devices for making the interior of this monster fish a more pleasant place to live in, but he has invented no device, no patent, no potent chemicals, no startling discoveries, no code of morals, no system of world government, no religious system whereby he can escape the sentence of death, for "salvation is of the Lord." We hear a great deal about the miracles of science, the conquering of disease, the increase of the span of life, but the real enemy, death, is still the same. The death rate of mankind has remained fixed and stable since the sentence of death was pronounced upon Adam six thousand years ago. The death rate is still the same — one death for every birth! The great question is not how to make the world a better place to live in, but how to get out of it, and be assured of a permanent place of safety.

Man's Inventions

There are many today who, without realizing the precariousness of our existence upon this old doomed world, seem to think that the place where we are, this world which lieth in wickedness, and represented by the belly of the whale, is still a pretty good place after all. Oh, yes, they admit all is not well, but then we will somehow improve it by and by. Ultimately we will abolish war, conquer disease, solve the problem of crime, and make a heaven out of this earth.

They are willing to admit that this old world needs some improvements in its social and economic and political arrangements to make it a true Utopia, but we are making progress. But are we really making progress? With the alarming increase in crime, broken homes, juvenile delinquency, apostasy and our hovering at the brink of total atomic destruction — we certainly are not making any progress. No, beloved, this is not the answer. It is no part of the mission of Christ to introduce social and political changes in the world, but to prepare men and women to escape the judgment which is rapidly overtaking us.

Not so Jonah

Jonah was not so foolish as to suppose that God's salvation would make him comfortable in the belly of the fish. He did not resign himself to his sojourn in that dark place, but sought a way out. How foolish it would have been for Jonah to say, "Well, this place is not what I might wish it to be, it certainly is not what it's cracked up to be, but I'll try and improve it, and make the best of the situation. If I could just clean it up a little, do a little decorating, and hang some pictures on these stomach walls, I wouldn't mind staying here for a while." Yet, men today will try and have us believe that this is the answer to our dilemma. No, my friend, the world over which death has universal dominion is not a good place to be in, and the best possible news to those who are in such a place is the news of a way out, through Jesus Christ. It is the good news of life from the dead.

THE RESURRECTION

This brings us to the resurrection of Jonah. No sooner had Jonah cried out, "Salvation is of the Lord," than God heard his prayer, and we read, immediately following, these interesting words:

> And the Lord spake unto the fish, and it vomited out Jonah upon the dry land (Jonah 2:10).

But let us not forget that it was not until after Jonah had ceased from his own works and efforts to extricate himself, and was willing to admit that only God could save him. It was when he cried, "Salvation is of the Lord." Man must die to all his own efforts and his own works, before he can be saved. When God creates anything, He always begins with nothing. He will not accept help from any other. It was so in the physical creation. "In the beginning God created." God had nothing but Himself to begin with, and so it is with the spiritual creation. God begins with nothing. In II Corinthians 5:17 we read:

> Therefore if any man be in Christ, he is a new creation: old things are passed away; behold, all things are become new.

It is an inviolable principle that there is no life without death. Jesus said in John,

> Except a corn of wheat fall into the ground and die, it abideth alone: but if it die, it bringeth forth much fruit (John 12:24).

Before God makes alive, He first kills. In Hannah's prayer in I Samuel she says:

> The Lord killeth, and maketh alive: he bringeth down to the grave, and bringeth up.
> The Lord maketh poor, and maketh rich: he bringeth low, and lifteth up.
> He raiseth up the poor out of the dust, and lifteth up the

beggar from the dunghill, to set them among princes, and to make them inherit the throne of glory (I Sam. 2:6-8).

Until man comes to the end of himself, and abandons the foolish, proud notion that he can do something to save himself, he cannot be saved. Paul tells us definitely in Romans,

But to him that worketh NOT, but believeth on him that justifieth the ungodly, his faith is counted for righteousness (Rom. 4:5).

Here then is the glorious truth of redemption. To all who will come as poor, hopeless, helpless, lost sinners, admitting that "salvation is of the Lord," God immediately grants salvation. No sooner had Jonah made his confession, "Salvation is of the Lord," than God immediately spoke to the fish, and Jonah was deposited safe and sound upon dry land.

A Complete Salvation

We would like to call your attention, before closing, to the place where the fish deposited Jonah. It was upon the DRY land. God's salvation is a perfect and a complete salvation. God never does a halfway job. The fish might have vomited Jonah up in the same place where he had swallowed him, and his case would have been no better. Or he might have vomited him up a half mile from the shore, or within swimming distance, in the event Jonah was able to swim. God could have commanded the fish to bring Jonah within reach of dry ground, and then leave it up to Jonah himself to wade the rest of the way under his own power. But no, God does not do things in this way; when He saves, He saves completely. Once the sinner abandons all hope of saving himself, God is ready to do all the rest. God does not save us, and then put us on our "own" after that, as to whether we will reach heaven safely or not. God places us in the position of complete safety, just as the fish vomited Jonah up on "dry" land.

What a parable of salvation this presents to us. God not only saves us, but has committed Himself to keep us as well. If we disobey, certainly He will chasten and judge us, as He did in the case of Jonah, but He will not forsake His own. Like Jonah, He will punish us and chasten us. He may even have to send storms and tempests. He may bring us to the very depths, but we are

> Confident of this very thing, that he which hath begun a good work in you will perform it until the day of Jesus Christ (Phil. 1:6).

GOOD NEWS FOR THE SINNER

And this indeed is good news for the sinner who may hesitate to come to Christ for salvation, because of the fear of his own weakness. Oftentimes when we have dealt with men and women for Christ, they have expressed their willingness to receive Christ, but they were fearful that they would not be able to hold out. Certainly it is true that no sinner is able to hold out by himself, but we have a Saviour who not only agrees to save us, but also "keep us" until the end. In case we stray away, like Jonah, the Lord may send painful experiences into our lives, but the Lord has promised that once we have committed our case into His hands, He will never leave us nor forsake us. The very fact the sinner is unable to keep himself is the greatest argument for coming to the only One who is able to keep.

In concluding this message, we would point you to the One and only Saviour, Who when He hung upon the Cross of Calvary, after having borne our sins in His own body on the tree, was able to say, "It is finished!" The work of salvation is a finished salvation. There is nothing the sinner can add or do to complete it. It must be received entirely as the free gift of God's grace. We must admit our utter unworthiness, and with Jonah be ready to cry out, "Salvation is of the Lord." Your salvation is ready and fully paid for, but you must accept it by faith. The only thing which will condemn the sinner is failure to accept God's finished work. God will not force it upon anyone.

> And the Spirit and the bride say, Come. And let him that heareth say, Come. And let him that is athirst come. And whosoever will, let him take the water of life freely (Rev. 22:17).

God Almighty Himself cannot save a man, if he refuses to accept God's remedy. At Calvary the Almighty God exhausted His omnipotence, and went to the infinite extreme of His omniscience to devise a plan of salvation for poor, lost, helpless sinners. God knows of no other way to save a sinner, than the way of grace through faith in the finished work of Christ. What folly then for man to try what God Himself has already given up as impossible; namely, to save a man without the blood of the Cross. No, that is not God's way. Here is God's way:

> For God so loved the world, that he gave his only begotten Son, that whosoever believeth in him should not perish, but have everlasting life (John 3:16).

Oh, sinner . . . stop trying . . . try trusting!

> Him that cometh to me I will in no wise cast out (John 6:37b).
> SALVATION IS OF THE LORD (Jonah 2:9).

Chapter Seventeen

JONAH – TYPE OF THE NATION OF ISRAEL

> And the word of the Lord came unto Jonah the second time, saying,
> Arise, go unto Nineveh, that great city, and preach unto it the preaching that I bid thee (Jonah 3:1,2).

SURPRISED, stunned and confused, Jonah sat on the shore of the Mediterranean Sea, after he had been resurrected and disgorged by the great fish. What would he do now? He was soon to know, for once again the Lord came and spoke to poor Jonah. Before taking up this second call of Jonah, we would like to remind you once again that the central lesson of Jonah is the story of the Death and the Resurrection of the Lord Jesus Christ. After Jonah had died in the belly of the fish, and had been resurrected, he became the great preacher to the Gentile city of Nineveh, which resulted in their repentance and conversion. So too, the Lord Jesus Christ by His Death and Resurrection became the Saviour of men and women everywhere. Today the Gospel is to every creature in fulfillment of the commission, "Go ye into all the world and preach the gospel to every creature."

BEFORE CALVARY

Before Jonah's experience in the fish, God dealt only with the nation of Israel, but after His Death and Resurrection, the message went out to the Gentiles, and they in turn believed. Even so, the message before the Cross and Death of the Lord Jesus Christ and His Resurrection was distinctly to the nation of Israel. His message to His apostles is clear:

These twelve Jesus sent forth, and commanded them, saying, Go not into the way of the Gentiles, and into any city of the Samaritans enter ye not:

But go rather to the lost sheep of the house of Israel (Matt. 10:5, 6).

But after the Cross of Calvary, the middle wall of partition is broken down between Jew and Gentile, and the message of "whosoever will" is to be preached universally throughout the world.

TYPE OF ISRAEL

Jonah is not only a clear type of the Lord Jesus Christ and of the backslider running away from God, but Jonah is also an unmistakable picture of the nation of Israel, of which he was a member. It is a remarkable affirmation of the words of God concerning the indestructibility of the miraculous nation of history — the nation of Israel. If it is a miracle that Jonah was preserved for three full days and nights in the depths of the sea, far more so is it a miracle that the nation of Israel has been miraculously, supernaturally, preserved for twenty-five hundred years of dispersion in the sea of the nations and in the place of impending death. God had made Himself known to Israel. He had clearly given His purpose in calling them from among the Gentiles. Unto this nation were "committed the oracles of God" (Rom. 3:2). Israel was chosen, set aside, elected, that the knowledge of the true God, Jehovah, might be preserved and known throughout the whole earth. God had told Abraham:

. . . and in thee shall all families of the earth be blessed (Gen. 12:3b).

But the people of Israel, like Jonah, failed in their great responsibility. They turned from God, and fell into disobedience, idolatry and sin. And so God sent upon them the very thing which befell the prophet Jonah. God also visited His people, and cast them overboard into the seething sea of the nations, and like Jonah, they have been swallowed up by the monster of race hatred, persecution and suffering. All of this had been predicted by the Lord. In Deuteronomy God had said:

> And the Lord shall scatter thee among all people, from the one end of the earth even unto the other; and there thou shalt serve other gods . . .
>
> And among these nations shalt thou find no ease, neither shall the sole of thy foot have rest: but the Lord shall give thee there a trembling heart, and failing of eyes, and sorrow of mind (Deut. 28:64, 65).

This description fits equally well the experience of Jonah, or the great picture of the nation of Israel.

SUPERNATURAL PRESERVATION

The great miracle of Jonah is his supernatural preservation from corruption. Though in the place of death and spiritually dead, the Hebrews have been preserved for all these centuries, and not destroyed. The greatest national miracle in all human history is the supernatural preservation and protection of a dispersed nation, persecuted and threatened in their sojourn among the nations, but never to be destroyed. Any other nation would have disappeared, would have been assimilated or destroyed in a few brief generations. But not so the nation of Israel, for they are to live once more in the land of Canaan, and like Jonah be deposited upon their own heritage.

All of this is taught in shadow in the experience of Jonah, and was minutely prophesied. In Deuteronomy 30 God gave a promise almost thirty-five hundred years ago:

> And it shall come to pass, when all these things are come upon thee, the blessing and the curse, which I have set before thee, and thou shalt call them to mind among all the nations, whither the Lord thy God hath driven thee,
>
> And shalt return unto the Lord thy God, and shalt obey his voice according to all that I command thee this day, thou and thy children, with all thine heart, and with all thy soul;
>
> That then the Lord thy God will turn thy captivity, and have compassion upon thee, and will return and gather thee

from all the nations, whither the Lord thy God hath scattered thee.

If any of thine be driven out unto the outmost parts of heaven, from thence will the Lord thy God gather thee, and from thence will he fetch thee:

And the Lord thy God will bring thee into the land which thy fathers possessed, and thou shalt possess it; and he will do thee good, and multiply thee above thy fathers (Deut. 30:1-5).

Or listen, if you please, to Isaiah 11:

And it shall come to pass in that day, that the Lord shall set his hand again the second time to recover the remnant of his people, which shall be left, from Assyria, and from Egypt, and from Pathros, and from Cush, and from Elam, and from Shinar, and from Hamath, and from the islands of the sea.

And he shall set up an ensign for the nations, and shall assemble the outcasts of Israel, and gather together the dispersed of Judah from the four corners of the earth (Isa. 11:11, 12).

And in Ezekiel 36, the prophet in speaking about the future of the nation of Israel, typified by the experience of Jonah, says this:

For I will take you from among the heathen, and gather you out of all countries, and will bring you into your own land.

Then will I sprinkle clean water upon you, and ye shall be clean: from all your filthiness, and from all your idols, will I cleanse you.

A new heart also will I give you, and a new spirit will I put within you: and I will take away the stony heart out of your flesh, and I will give you an heart of flesh.

And I will put my spirit within you, and cause you to walk in my statutes, and ye shall keep my judgments, and do them.

And ye shall dwell in the land that I gave to your fathers; and ye shall be my people, and I will be your God (Ezek. 36:24-28).

IN THE LAND

During this past decade we have seen the beginning of the fulfillment of all these prophecies in the establishment of a nation in the land of Palestine, and significantly called "Israel." They are there after centuries of wandering among the nations, yet supernaturally preserved. They have already as a political entity been deposited on their own land. This is not the complete fulfillment of prophecy, but the beginning of its fulfillment. The nation will yet experience the full possession of all the land of Canaan, and be spiritually revived and become the herald of salvation to the whole world. How near that day must be! The fig tree has already budded; it is flowering profusely. Soon the fruit will appear.

Jonah then is a picture of Israel, disobedient at first, cast among the nations, swallowed but never digested, and ultimately when Jesus comes, to be resurrected as a nation, placed in their own land to become, like Jonah, God's own messengers for the salvation of the Gentiles. They shall, like Jonah, be God's witnesses, and today their presence in the world stands as the greatest testimony to the truthfulness of God's Word in a wicked world. They cannot be destroyed. Pharaoh could not drown them, Nebuchadnezzar was unable to burn them, Haman could not exterminate them, the lions would not eat them, and the whale could not digest them. As Jonah is a miracle, so the nation of Israel typified by Jonah is God's miracle nation, and soon they shall be brought to their own land and fulfill the purpose for which they were called in the covenant of Abraham by the Lord.

Type of the Lord Jesus

We recommend for your careful study this intriguing and interesting account of Jonah as a type of the nation to which he belonged. When the hour of God comes, He will speak to the nations that have swallowed up and afflicted His people, and then they will deliver them up and deposit them upon their own land. This is in process right today, and is already far advanced. Israel will be reborn out of the waters of death, and will take its God-appointed place at the head of the nations. And then, as Jonah fulfilled God's commission to the

Gentile city of Nineveh after he had been, so to speak, born again from the dead, so Israel will in the coming age, make known the name of Jehovah to the nations of the earth.

> Yea, many people and strong nations shall come to seek the Lord of hosts in Jerusalem, and to pray before the Lord.
>
> Thus saith the Lord of hosts; In those days it shall come to pass, that ten men shall take hold out of all languages of the nations, even shall take hold of the skirt of him that is a Jew, saying, We will go with you: for we have heard that God is with you (Zech. 8:22, 23).

There is then probably no clearer picture of God's eternal program for this miracle nation of history. We repeat, the greatest international miracle of history is the history of the nation of destiny, the nation of Israel. But all of this brings us face to face with the fulfillment of prophecy and the promise of the Lord's soon return. Our Lord was asked by His disciples,

> When shall these things be? and what shall be the sign of thy coming, and of the end of the world? (Matt. 24:3).

He gave a large number of signs, and in the very middle of it, He reminds us that when the fig tree, which is the nation of Israel, begins to bud and to blossom, then we may know that it is at our very doors. Surely the fig tree today is not only budding, but it has burst into bloom, and we believe that soon the coming of the Lord will take place, and then Israel shall become the fruitful vine of the Lord. In view of all this, how imperative to send out the message of redemption, and to plead with lost sinners to receive the Lord Jesus Christ before it is forever too late.

Chapter Eighteen

BEFORE AND AFTER CALVARY

> Arise, go to Nineveh . . . and cry against it (Jonah 1:2).
> Arise, go unto Nineveh . . . and preach unto it (Jonah 3:2).

THE prophet Jonah received two calls from the Lord to preach in the city of Nineveh. The first call Jonah disobeyed; the second call he fulfilled. Between the two calls, Jonah had a most gruesome experience, dying in the belly of a fish, and then being miraculously resurrected and deposited upon the dry land. Superficial and hasty reading of these two calls shows no difference in their content, and yet they are quite different. The difference lies in the change of one single word. The word, "against," in the first call (Jonah 1:2) is changed to "unto" in the second call in Jonah 3:2. In the first instance Jonah is commanded to preach AGAINST the city, and it was a message of judgment and condemnation. But in the second call, Jonah is not commanded to preach AGAINST Nineveh, but UNTO it. And this time it is not a message of doom and judgment but a message of grace and mercy and a call to repentance.

LAW AND GRACE

We ask the question, therefore, Why the difference in the two calls? What is the reason the first call was a message of judgment, against the city of Nineveh, while the second call resulted in repentance and salvation for these Gentiles? We have the answer in the events which transpired between the two calls. The first call was BEFORE the death and resurrection of Jonah. The second call was AFTER his experience

142

in the belly of the fish. The difference between doom and mercy was Jonah's experience in the fish, as a type of the Gospel of the Lord Jesus Christ.

We know that Jonah is a type of our Saviour in His Death and Burial and Resurrection. Before the Cross men lived in the age of law — after the Cross it became the age of grace. Before the Cross the ministry of justice and death reigned, but now after Calvary the message is mercy and life. Between the age of law and grace stands the Cross of Calvary. Between death and life stands the crucified Saviour.

We are not told what Jonah was commanded to preach in his first commission, but we know it was AGAINST them, and therefore, it was a message of judgment. We read nothing about forty days of probation, or the offer of salvation if they repented, as we have it in the second call. It is a picture, therefore, of the threatenings and judgments of Sinai without any hope for the sinner. But notice the message AFTER the death and the resurrection of Jonah as a type of the Lord Jesus Christ. It was:

> Yet forty days, and Nineveh shall be overthrown (Jonah 3:4).

On the surface this still sounds like a message of judgment, but in reality it is a message of grace. God gives the Ninevites another chance. He gives them forty days in which to turn to the living God. We have already seen that the number forty is the number of probation, or testing. Jonah did predict the overthrow of the city, but it was "conditioned" upon their acceptance or rejection of the message of Jonah, within the space of forty days. This is evident from the way God spared them, when before the forty days were up, they repented of their sins.

There could be no message of mercy until justice had been satisfied. Before Jonah's typical death and resurrection, the only message he had was a message of judgment. Jonah was a sinner, and the sinner must die, and only after the penalty for sin is paid could God be satisfied. This is the case with every one of us. We have sinned, and deserve eternal death. But God wanted to save us, and so He sent Jesus to die in our place. He became our "Jonah," and by His death for us God's justice and the demands of the law were fully satisfied, and now whosoever will believe may be saved.

NOT LAW BUT GRACE

Yet how the proud heart of man rebels against this message of grace. How loathe and slow he is to admit that he is hopeless and helpless, and that without simple grace he cannot be saved. Like the sailors of Jonah's time, men will not accept God's remedy until they have tried every device which they possibly could invent. And yet the Bible tells us that perfect, unbroken obedience to the law of God is demanded. One single sin is sufficient to condemn us.

> For as many as are of the works of the law are under the curse: for it is written, Cursed is every one that continueth not in all things which are written in the book of the law to do them (Gal. 3:10).

Notice please every word of this important verse. No other verse sums up the purpose of the law like this one. Note the first word, CURSED. That is all the law can do to a SINNER. And a sinner under the curse is one who CONTINUES NOT IN ALL THINGS WRITTEN IN THE LAW. How can we mistake those words? "Cursed is EVERYONE that CONTINUETH NOT IN ALL THINGS WRITTEN in the law to do them." The law demands PERFECTION. Nothing less will do. It demands that the sinner NEVER SLIP ONCE. Keeping the law part of the time is not enough. It demands PERFECTION. And everyone, according to this verse, who does not uninterruptedly CONTINUE to do ALL THE LAW is under the curse. Need I remind you then that ALL ARE UNDER the curse of the law, since no man except Jesus Christ has ever lived or ever will live who has CONTINUED IN ALL THINGS WRITTEN in the book of the law. That is just why Jesus had to die. That very fact, that no man ever did keep or could keep God's holy law, NECESSITATED the death of Christ. If there lived one single individual who could have kept God's law perfectly, there would have been no need for Christ's coming, since then it would be proven that man COULD be saved by the righteousness of the law. But Paul says in Galatians,

> I do not frustrate the grace of God: for IF RIGHTEOUSNESS COME BY THE LAW, then Christ IS DEAD IN VAIN (Gal. 2:21).

THE LAW CONDEMNS

When God gave the law on the tables of stone on Mount Sinai, He knew that no human being could keep that holy law. Yea, He knew that no one ever would. Nay, more, God never expected a single sinner to keep His law. That was not the purpose of the law. God gave the law to PROVE that man could not be saved by LAW WORKS, that it might convince mankind of the need of the grace of God, and get them ready to accept the grace of God in Christ Jesus. The law is perfect; that is why imperfect men cannot keep it. The law is holy; that is why sinners are condemned by it. The law is just, and therefore, cannot show mercy to the guilty, for that would be in violation of its righteousness and justice. The law can only show the nature of sin. The law condemns, and says,

> Cursed is everyone that continueth not in ALL THINGS written in the book of the law to do them (Gal. 3:10).

REDEEMED BY CHRIST

Now notice:

> Christ hath redeemed us from the curse of the law, being made a curse for us: for it is written, Cursed is every one that hangeth on a tree (Gal. 3:13).

Christ has redeemed us from THE CURSE of the law. The CURSE of the law is the penalty of the LAW, even death. Christ by His death has delivered us from ETERNAL DEATH, the penalty of a broken law. A law without penalties is powerless. The only thing that makes a law something to be feared is the fact that it demands punishment. That is what legislators mean when they say PUTTING TEETH IN THE LAW, making the penalty so severe that men will be forced to keep it. But when the penalty is removed, the teeth are taken out. To every believer, then, the penalty of the law has been met by the Saviour. He bore our sins in His own body on the tree. Jesus said:

> He that heareth my word, and believeth on him that sent me, hath everlasting life, and shall not come into condemnation; but is passed from death unto life (John 5:24).

To accept Christ is to be free from the law with its curse and its condemnation. To accept Christ is to have ETERNAL LIFE. Galatians 3:17 guarantees the eternal truth of our salvation. Paul illustrates in this verse the fact that ONCE UNDER THE GRACE OF GOD, the law has no more dominion. He contrasts the covenant of grace with Abraham with the law of works given 430 years later. The fact that Israel failed under the law does not annul God's covenant of grace, made before with Abraham. Notice the words:

> And this I say, that the covenant, that was confirmed before of God in Christ, the law, which was four hundred and thirty years after, cannot disannul, that it should make the promise of none effect.
> For if the inheritance be of the law, it is no more of promise: but God gave it to Abraham by promise (Gal. 3:17, 18).

Israel was under God's covenant of grace, and still is, and ever will be, for God's covenant which He swore by HIMSELF cannot be broken. The fact that Abraham's seed, Israel, BROKE HIS LAW, brought upon them God's discipline but it does not annul God's covenant of grace. All this is given as an illustration for us. If we are saved, we are saved by grace, and grace alone. Our salvation depends on what Jesus did; not what WE do. It depends not on what we feel, but what JESUS felt for us. It depends not on OUR FAITHFULNESS, but on His faithfulness. As it was with Israel, so it is with us. Disobedience will bring God's chastening, but His covenant of grace still keeps us. God is faithful; He cannot deny Himself. For the believer to be disobedient is to invite God's disciplinary dealings. Witness the experience of Jonah the disobedient prophet. Israel found it out for the past two thousand years. They have been scattered out of the land, because they broke God's law, but they are still God's covenant people, and will once again be regathered and blessed. Our "salvation" depends on grace. Our "enjoyment" of salvation depends on our behavior. Our justification is by faith; our rewards will be by works. Your eternal life is GOD'S GIFT, and does not depend on anything you do. It is all of grace.

SAVED BY GRACE

Oh, my friends, have you received eternal life by the grace of God? Unless you have, you are still lost. The plan of salvation is so simple that most people stumble over it. They do not realize that it is a finished work, and is to be had for the taking. Satan has tried hard to delude you into believing that you must do something yourself. Don't you believe him, but believe the Word which says·

But to him that worketh not, but believeth on him that justifieth the ungodly, his faith is counted for righteousness (Rom. 4:5).

Not by works of righteousness which we have done, but according to his mercy he saved us, by the washing of regeneration, and renewing of the Holy Ghost (Titus 3:5).

Chapter Nineteen

DOES GOD EVER CHANGE HIS MIND?

Does God ever change His mind? What does it mean when the Scripture says that God "repented" of what He had done? Does not the Scripture also state that with God there is no "variableness, neither shadow of turning" (Jas. 1:17)? In Malachi we read,

> For I am the Lord, I change not (Mal. 3:6).

Again, in I Samuel,

> And also the Strength of Israel will not lie nor repent: for he is not a man, that he should repent (I Sam. 15:29).

From these Scriptures it is clear that God never changes His mind, for

> Known unto God are all his works from the beginning of the world (Acts 15:18).

The immutability of God is an attribute which is essential to His being. We could not trust a God Who changes His mind, since He knows all things from eternity. Yet in Jonah 3 we are told that God repented of the evil He had pronounced upon the city of Nineveh.

Jonah had preached his message of judgment, "Yet forty days and Nineveh shall be overthrown." Hearing this, and believing the sign, the king's heart was touched, and he proclaimed a fast and called the people to repentance. We read:

> So the people of Nineveh believed God, and proclaimed a fast, and put on sackcloth, from the greatest of them even to the least of them.

148

For word came unto the king of Nineveh, and he arose from his throne, and he laid his robe from him, and covered him with sackcloth, and sat in ashes.

And he caused it to be proclaimed and published through Nineveh by the decree of the king and his nobles, saying, Let neither man nor beast, herd nor flock, taste any thing: let them not feed, nor drink water:

But let man and beast be covered with sackcloth, and cry mightily unto God: yea, let them turn every one from his evil way, and from the violence that is in their hands.

Who can tell if God will turn and repent, and turn away from his fierce anger, that we perish not?

And God saw their works, that they turned from their evil way; and God repented of the evil, that he had said he would do unto them; and he did it not (Jonah 3:5-10).

Now is it possible for us to harmonize the many, many statements in God's Word, which we have quoted concerning the unchangeableness and the immutability of God, with this statement in Jonah that "God repented," and changed His mind? Does man's conduct cause God to change His mind? We have another similar passage in Genesis 6:

And God saw that the wickedness of man was great in the earth, and that every imagination of the thoughts of his heart was only evil continually.

And it repented the Lord that he had made man on the earth, and it grieved him at his heart (Gen. 6:5, 6).

Before attempting an explanation of this seeming contradiction, let me state that we believe with all our heart in the absolute sovereignty and immutability of our God. He is God, and as such is a Supreme Being in all His actions and attributes. He does not have to give an account of what He does to any mere man. As a sovereign God He had a plan from all eternity. He knew exactly what He was going to do, so that there would never be any need for changing His plan, for God cannot be surprised.

The repentance of Nineveh, therefore, did not cause God to change His mind. Rather it was God's way of carrying out His purpose for Nineveh. God knew that Nineveh would repent. He wanted Nineveh to repent. He planned and purposed that they should be spared, and to bring this about, He sent Jonah to preach to them, in order that His sovereign purpose in saving Nineveh and bringing them to repentance might be carried out.

GOD'S WAY IN JUDGMENT

In order to accomplish this predetermined, predestinated result, He declared impending judgment upon them. This was God's means to drive them to repentance, so God might spare them as He had intended it. The statement, therefore, that God repented, does not imply a change of mind or purpose, but rather that God had heard the prayer of the Ninevites to save them.

The word for repentance in the Old Testament is *nacham*. It comes from a Hebrew root, meaning "to sigh" or to "pant," or to "groan." Thus the word came to mean, "to lament, to grieve, and to pity." The verse, therefore, may be freely translated, that God was "grieved" over the judgment upon Nineveh, and "pitied" them in their doom, and, therefore, He sent them the message to save them. The word, *nacham*, translated "to repent," is used some forty times in the Old Testament, and in almost every case refers to repentance on the part of God. In all instances, it means that God was grieved at man's condition, and in pity offered them His salvation. In the New Testament, where the word, "repentance," is used, it refers in almost every instance to human repentance, and implies a radical change of mind, and a turning from sin to God. This is also illustrated in Nineveh's repentance. They not only changed their minds, but their hearts, and proved it by their works. We have it in the record in Jonah 3:8.

> But let man and beast be covered with sackcloth, and cry mightily unto God: yea, let them turn every one from his evil way, and from the violence that is in their hands.

This was genuine repentance, proven by "works of repentance."

There are two kinds of human repentance — true and false. False repentance is sorrow over the "result" of sin; true repentance is sorrow over sin itself. These two kinds of repentance are given in II Corinthians:

> For godly sorrow worketh repentance to salvation not to be repented of: but the sorrow of the world worketh death (II Cor. 7:10).

True repentance is known by its fruits. The Ninevites "turned from their evil ways," and therefore produced fruits. Jesus said to the Pharisees:

> Bring forth therefore fruits worthy of repentance (Luke 3:8).

Paul the apostle preached this in his testimony before Agrippa in Acts when he said:

> . . . that they should repent and turn to God, and do works meet for repentance (Acts 26:20b).

So much for human repentance. When the Bible states that God repents, however, it cannot mean the same as human repentance. God does not have to be sorry for anything He has done. He does not turn from His evil doings, for He is perfect and holy and sinless.

We repeat, therefore, that when we read that God repented, it was God's way of saying that His purpose had been accomplished. He had said, "Yet forty days and Nineveh shall be destroyed." Then Nineveh repented. That was the purpose of the message of judgment which God had sent through the prophet Jonah. It was true, of course, that IF Nineveh did not repent in forty days, it would be destroyed. But the IF applied to man — not to God. The condition was man's, not God's. God already knew that they would repent, and so He used language adapted and accommodated to our understanding when we read that "God repented." It literally means God "pitied" them, and so made salvation for them possible.

FORTY DAYS

All of this, I think, is made clear by the fact that God gave them forty days in which to repent. If it had been God's original purpose to destroy Nineveh, He could have done it immediately, but instead, He set a deadline — yet forty days. God sets a deadline for sinners too, and when that point is reached, God acts, either in salvation or in judgment. God also set a deadline for the antediluvians in Noah's day. In Genesis 6:3 we read about this deadline:

> And the Lord said, My spirit shall not always strive with man, for that he also is flesh: yet his days shall be an hundred and twenty years.

Here then we have God setting a deadline of one hundred and twenty years, and when the end of that time came, and they had not repented, God's original foreknown judgment fell upon the wicked world. In the case of Nineveh, however, they repented, and God's foreknown purpose in saving them was accomplished.

Yet forty days! God sets a limit on man's days of opportunity, and says, "yet forty days." While God knew just what they would do, yet from the human standpoint it all depended upon their response. We cannot explain these things, but we are to believe them. We cannot with our limited minds reconcile God's sovereignty in election and predestination, and man's free will. Neither is this necessary. It is God's business to elect; it is ours to believe. We can well leave the election with God, and do our part, which is to believe. It is not our business to do the electing, nor to question God concerning it. It is our business to believe, and when we do, we may be sure that God does not fail to do His part. Stop being concerned about God's sovereign choice, and do your part in receiving Christ, and you may rest assured that God will be faithful. If you would really like to be saved, and know whether you have been elected of God, then simply believe His Word, receive His Son, and Trust Him who said in John,

> All that the Father giveth me shall come to me (John 6:37a).

That is God's part. With this you have nothing to do, but the last part of the verse belongs to you:

> And him that cometh to me I will in no wise cast out (John 6:37b).

That is the part that man must fulfill. You must come, and when you do, you have the promise that He will receive you. And then after you come, you find to your joy that:

> Ye have not chosen me, but I have chosen you, and ordained you, that ye should go and bring forth fruit, and that your fruit should remain (John 15:16).

You must come, but there is a limit also. Nineveh was given forty days — no longer. And you too must come within your "forty days" of opportunity. Once the time is up, it will be forever too late. Clearly we are told in Hebrews,

> It is appointed unto men once to die, and after this the judgment (Heb. 9:27).

There was a time when you were appointed to be born, over which you had no control. You came by divine appointment. Even so, there is a time appointed for you to die, about which you too have no control, and no choice. When that hour comes, all the skill of man cannot stop the hand of death. If the Lord tarries, there will come a certain moment when each of us will have to leave this life. As sure as we were born, so surely we must die. When is that moment for you? For some of you it will be today; for many more it will be this week. Your "forty days" may be up at any time. For some of you the forty days of probation are in the last minutes, and it is thirty-nine days, twenty-three hours, and fifty-nine minutes before the deadline fixed for you. Will you like the Ninevites repent and be saved, or like the sinners in Noah's day, cross the deadline and perish in the judgment of God. It is still the accepted time. You may cross the line at any time, and then it will be forever too late. Will you not, therefore, stop right now before another moment passes, and call upon God to save you, and then believe His promise?

For whosoever shall call upon the name of the Lord shall
be saved (Rom. 10:13).

There is a line by us unseen, that crosses every path;
The hidden boundary between God's patience and His wrath.
Oh, where is this mysterious bourne, by which our path is
crossed;
Beyond which God Himself hath sworn, that he who goes
is lost.
One answer from the skies is sent, Ye who from God depart;
While it is called today, repent, and harden not your heart.

Yet forty days, and Nineveh shall be overthrown (Jonah 3:4).

Chapter Twenty

A VINE, A WORM, AND AN EAST WIND

> So Jonah went out of the city, and sat on the east side of the
> city, and there made him a booth, and sat under it in the
> shadow, till he might see what would become of the city (Jonah
> 4:5).

OF all the lessons we may gather from the Book of Jonah,
one of the most outstanding is the marvelous demonstration of
the mercy and the grace of God. Mercy and grace are inter-
woven throughout the entire narrative. God had mercy on
the poor, frightened sailors caught in the violent storm. God
had mercy on the people of a great and wicked city when
they repented and turned to the Lord.

But the most amazing evidence of God's grace is in His
dealing with Jonah himself. As we read the record of this
fickle, selfish, bigoted, temperamental servant of the Lord,
we stand in awe at the longsuffering patience and kindness
of God. How patiently and tenderly God dealt with him when
he fled the path of duty. How wonderfully God delivered
him from the belly of the fish and gave him his second
commission to preach to Nineveh.

But the most astounding demonstration of God's grace
toward Jonah, we find in the closing chapter of the book. It is
the picture of a disappointed, disgruntled, fault-finding child
of God, arguing with and even criticizing God for the way
He dealt with sinners. Jonah must have preached God's
judgment upon the Ninevites, the traditional enemies of Israel,
with a certain degree of delight and satisfaction. He was
pleased to think God was going to destroy these pagans, and

155

when they repented, and God in mercy spared them, he was
sorely displeased.

KNEW IT ALL BEFORE

Jonah knew that God was a merciful God. We now find
out, in Jonah 4:2, why he had disobeyed God in the first place,
and had fled to Tarshish. Not until we reach this verse in
Jonah are we informed of the real reason for Jonah's backsliding. He knew that if he preached judgment to Nineveh,
and they repented, that God would save them and he would
appear before them as a false preacher. Listen to the record:

> But it displeased Jonah exceedingly, (Nineveh's repentance
> and God's mercy upon them) and he was very angry.
> And he prayed unto the Lord, and said I pray thee, O Lord,
> was not this my saying, when I was yet in my country? There-
> fore I fled before unto Tarshish: for I knew that thou art a
> gracious God, and merciful, slow to anger, and of great kind-
> ness, and repentest thee of the evil.
> Therefore now, O Lord, take, I beseech thee, my life from
> me: for it is better for me to die than to live.
> Then said the Lord, Doest thou well to be angry? (Jonah
> 4:1-4)

One is surprised that God did not answer Jonah's prayer and
slay him on the spot. He certainly deserved nothing less.
But Jonah did not yet know the depths of God's grace and
mercy, and so God instead of taking his life as Jonah had
requested, continues to deal with him, to teach him his
lesson. He must be taught the value of a human soul. He
must learn that which Jesus later taught:

> For what is a man profited, if he shall gain the whole world,
> and lose his own soul? (Matt. 16:26)

So we find Jonah busy building a little booth for his personal
comfort, while awaiting the doom of the city. Jonah was
greatly interested in his own material comfort. He could
sleep in the midst of a storm, and loll at ease under a booth,
amid impending judgment. But a man made booth was

inadequate to give the needed shelter to the prophet, and so the
Lord caused a gourd to grow up over the booth. The word
in the original indicates a wild cucumber vine of poisonous
nature, probably the same poison gourds mentioned in II Kings,
chapter 4. Jonah was glad, but it was of short duration, for
God prepared a worm which in a night ate at the root of the
vine, and caused it to wither away, leaving Jonah without
shelter. And then God sent a sultry east wind which smote
Jonah upon his head (probably bald) until he fainted, and
once again Jonah wished in himself to die, and said, "It is
better for me to die than live."

What Is the Meaning?

Now what is the meaning of this strange account? What
significance have this poison gourd and this hungry worm?
There is one lesson we cannot miss, for God Himself gives the
interpretation. Jonah must be taught the value of the human
soul. Listen to God's Word to Jonah:

> Then said the Lord, Thou hast had pity on the gourd, for the
> which thou hast not laboured, neither madest it grow; which
> came up in a night, and perished in a night:
> And should not I spare Nineveh, that great city, wherein are
> more than sixscore thousand persons that cannot discern between
> their right hand and their left hand; and also much cattle?
> (Jonah 4:10, 11)

Jonah must learn the relative value of the temporal and
the eternal, the material and the spiritual. Jonah was so
occupied with his own comfort, the booth, and the gourd, he
forgot the plight of poor, lost souls in the city of Nineveh.
But there is even more here. The booth was the work of
Jonah's hands; the gourd was the result of natural growth. To
depend on these is building on sand, and to demonstrate the
transciency of temporal things, God prepared a worm to
destroy the gourd overnight.

It is significant that it was a worm which destroyed the
gourd. The word translated "worm" is *to-law,* and is the

identical word translated in many other places as the word, "scarlet" or "crimson." In the familiar passage in Isaiah 1:18, "though your sins be as scarlet, they shall be as white as snow; though they be red like crimson, they shall be as wool," the word translated "crimson" is the identical word translated "worm" in Jonah 4. We might, therefore, translate the phrase, "though they be red like a worm;" or on the other hand, the verse in Jonah could be translated, "God prepared a crimson." The reason is, that the words "crimson," "scarlet" and "worm" are all translations of one and the same word in Hebrew, to-law. There seems to be little connection until we realize that the original really means a "crimson worm." This worm was a red worm from which a precious deep red dye was made, and used to color the drapings of the tabernacle, as well as the clothing of the High Priest. The word is, therefore, applied to the worm itself, as well as to its color. In dozens of instances, especially in Exodus, the word is translated "scarlet," but a literal rendering would be "scarlet worm." Returning to Jonah's account, therefore, we may render it:

But God prepared a "red-worm," when the morning rose the next day (Jonah 4:7).

We know that the scarlet color in the construction of the tabernacle pointed forward to the blood of the Lord Jesus Christ. The scarlet cord of Rahab the harlot of Jericho was also colored by the dye extracted from the body of an insect. But there is another place where the "worm" seems to have a prophetic picture. In Psalm 22, the psalmist David writes prophetically concerning the sufferings and death of the Lord Jesus Christ. It opens with the prophecy of the very words that Jesus would utter on the Cross:

My God, my God, why hast thou forsaken me? (Ps. 22:1)

The rest of the psalm is a detailed description of the agonies of Christ on the Cross, His suffering, His sweat, His thirst, the parting of His garments, the piercing of His hands and feet, all these leave no doubt that it refers to the Lord Jesus. And in the course of this psalm, we hear him saying, prophetically:

> But I am a worm, and no man; a reproach of men, and despised of the people.
> All they that see me laugh me to scorn: they shoot out the lip, they shake the head, saying,
> He trusted on the Lord that he would deliver him, seeing he delighted in him (Ps. 22:6-8).

We would have you notice that our Lord here declares "I am a worm." It is again the same word, meaning a "scarlet worm." The reference clearly is to Calvary, and His death on the Cross. There He indeed became a "worm," dying between two criminals, despised and rejected of men. He became the "scarlet worm" of Calvary. It is a scene of blood, blood oozing from His skin in great agonizing drops, blood from His lacerated back, blood from His brow, pierced with thorns, blood from His hands and His feet, blood from His pierced side.

This we believe to be the worm which smote the gourd which sheltered Jonah's naked head. Jonah had sought comfort in a man made booth, and a fragile plant of the earth. Significantly it was a poison gourd. He placed his hope for comfort in the frail work of his own hands, and the transient shade of a perishing gourd. And God comes and levels his frail shelter with a worm — a blood red worm. We believe there are at least two lessons here.

Picture of Calvary

As the worm destroyed the gourd, so Calvary negates all the efforts of man to provide his own shelter. Calvary is death to all man's efforts to provide for his own salvation. It is death to all efforts to be saved by the works of the law.

> For if righteousness come by the law, then Christ is dead in vain (Gal. 2:21b).

Calvary is God's answer to all human effort to save self. As the slain sacrifice in Genesis 3:21 and God's provision of the bloody skins to cover Adam and Eve was the answer to man's fig leaf garments, and as the "red-worm" in Jonah was God's answer to Jonah's efforts to provide himself a shelter, so Calvary is God's answer to all of man's efforts to save himself. He must learn to abandon all his own work, and say:

> Nothing in my hand I bring;
> Simply to Thy Cross I cling.

Man must still learn the humbling but indispensable lesson that salvation can only be received by grace through the work of Calvary without the deeds of the law.

> But to him that worketh not, but believeth on him that justifieth the ungodly, his faith is counted for righteousness (Rom. 4:5).

LOOK TO CALVARY

There is a second lesson in the "red worm" of Jonah's gourd. Jonah is reminded of the love of God. Since we believe the "red worm" which stripped Jonah of all his own righteousness was a picture of Christ on the Cross, we see the supreme demonstration of the love of God for sinners. Jonah would have rejoiced to see Nineveh destroyed, and so God reminds him how ungodlike his action is. He points him in figure by means of a worm to the love of God, and the awful price He was willing to pay for man's redemption. And until we see the magnitude, the height and the depth of God's love at Calvary, we too will remain indifferent to the plight of the lost. Oh, how God loved the sinner. Even though like Jonah, man rebels against God, finds fault with Him, disobeys Him, and even blames Him, God in longsuffering mercy not only bears with him, but provides a salvation for him by giving His Son to die on the Cross, until prophetically he cries, "I am a worm."

Come with me, therefore, in closing, once more to Calvary. There hangs the Son of God, the Creator of the universe, in shame and nakedness. Blood streams from His head, His hands, His back, His brow, His feet. The pitiless sun beats mercilessly upon His body. Round about Him stands a howling, shrieking, blood-thirsty crowd, gloating in glee over His suffering. They taunt Him, revile Him, mock Him, and laugh Him to scorn. He could have called fire down from heaven and damned them all into hell, which would have been just and proper. But instead, He voluntarily remains on that Cross in order that by His own blood and death He might redeem the very ones who thirsted for His innocent blood. Can you stand there and realize that,

> Was it for crimes that I have done,
> He groaned upon the tree?
> Amazing pity! grace unknown!
> And love beyond degree!

Oh, Jonah, why not arise from your miserable hillside seat, and rush into the city and rejoice with those who have been spared and tell to all who will hear the glad, glad story of Him who said,

> I am a worm . . . despised, and rejected of men; a man of sorrows, and acquainted with grief (Ps. 22:6; Isa. 53:3).
>
> But he was wounded for our transgressions, he was bruised for our iniquities: the chastisement of our peace was upon him; and with his stripes we are healed (Isa. 53:5).

Have you been building a booth of your own works, hoping to find under it shelter from the flames of hell? Have you taken refuge under a gourd of transient, fleeting, worldly comfort and satisfaction? Then abandon your own efforts, arise and come to Calvary and be saved.

> For whosoever shall call upon the name of the Lord shall be saved (Rom. 10:13).

Chapter Twenty-one

THE SIN OF BIGOTRY

JONAH was a religious bigot. He was a preacher, but he hoped his preaching would not take effect, and was deeply disappointed and angry when God saved sinners who repented at his preaching. Jonah was not angry because sinners repented, but angry because a certain "class" of sinners had been saved. He would have rejoiced in their salvation, if they had belonged to his own crowd, and his own nation, and his own group, but he found it hard to rejoice in the salvation of his enemies. Jonah was a Hebrew, a member of God's chosen nation, and the Ninevites to whom he was sent were Gentile dogs, enemies and oppressors of his beloved people.

Because of this Jonah tried to run away from his job, and it took a storm and three days in the belly of the fish to make him ready to do the job which God had committed unto him. Apparently Jonah preached with great gusto and enthusiasm as he pronounced "judgment" upon his enemies, glorying in the conviction that they would soon be getting what they deserved.

THE GREAT SURPRISE

But to Jonah's dismay and disappointment, the people of Nineveh repented, and God saved them. This greatly annoyed and displeased the prophet, and we read the amazing record:

> But it displeased Jonah exceedingly, and he was very angry.
> And he prayed unto the Lord, and said, I pray thee, O Lord, was not this my saying, when I was yet in my country? Therefore I fled before unto Tarshish: for I knew that thou art a gracious God, and merciful, slow to anger, and of great kindness, and repentest thee of the evil.

162

> Therefore now, O Lord, take, I beseech thee, my life from
> me; for it is better for me to die than to live.
> Then said the Lord, Doest thou well to be angry? (Jonah
> 4:1-4)

Poor, poor Jonah! Down in the dumps and wanting to die!
Instead of rejoicing in the salvation of these sinners to whom
he had preached, he is disappointed and angry. What an
evil disease is bigotry. There are a number of reasons for
Jonah's displeasure. First of all, his pride had been injured. He
had not expected the repentance of the city at all, and now
that they had turned to the Lord, he felt that his ministry
had been discredited. He had predicted judgment and now the
people had lost respect for him, because what he had predicted
had not come to pass. Evidently Jonah had only preached
certain judgment, and not God's love and mercy.

But the real reason for his anger was just selfish bigotry.
He was interested only in his own nation of Israel. Jonah
held the bigoted notion that they alone were God's people
and worthy of His care. Because the Ninevites were not
Hebrews, he felt no interest in them, and would just as
soon leave them alone to be lost. Now I am sure that all
of you are ready to condemn this attitude of Jonah, and
castigate him for his narrow-mindedness. But let us not be too
hasty in our condemnation, for in so doing, we might condemn ourselves. We call it "bigotry" in Jonah, but what about
"sectarianism" among us. After all, "sectarianism" is nothing
but bigotry. We think that our own church, our own de-
nomination, is the only true church, and we have all the truth,
and refuse fellowship with others who cannot subscribe to
all our interpretations, our do's and don'ts, and hair-splitting
dogmas. We build denominational fences, formulate exclusive
creeds and dogmas, and refuse fellowship to others who may
differ on inconsequential details. What else is this but bigotry?

Are you interested more in making members for your
church than in saving sinners for Christ? Can you rejoice in a
great revival in the church across the street, while God has

not visited your church in the same measure? Are you as interested in the poor lost heathen in Africa or Asia as you are in the program of your own group?

SECTARIANISM IS SIN

Some people love their church more than they do the Lord. They would hinder and obstruct others who preach the Gospel, just because they do not represent their own assembly. By criticism, hairsplitting, gossip and urging of people to support only their own little sect, they are keeping sinners from coming to Christ. Oh, how it must displease our Lord! Jesus condemned this attitude severely while He was here on the earth. On one occasion one of His disciples came to Him, saying:

> Master, we saw one casting out devils in thy name; and we forbad him, because he followeth not with us (Luke 9:49).

What a tragedy to let this poor man suffer, possessed of a devil, rather than have the devils cast out by someone outside of their own little group. Notice, therefore, the words of the Lord Jesus Christ:

> Forbid him not: for he that is not against us is for us (Luke 9:50).

JONAH'S LESSON

This lesson Jonah must learn. Instead of rejoicing in the doom of those to whom he preached, he should be rejoicing and praising God for their salvation. But Jonah was not only proud and bigoted, he was intensely selfish. While waiting and hoping for God's judgment to fall on Nineveh, he was far more concerned with his own comfort than the salvation of others. With this picture of Jonah the book ends, rather abruptly:

> So Jonah went out of the city, and sat on the east side of the city, and there made him a booth, and sat under it in the shadow, till he might see what would become of the city (Jonah 4:5).

All Jonah thought of now was his own comfort. He cared not for the fate of a doomed city. He thought only of his own temporal and material comfort and ease, and so God proceeds to teach Jonah a much needed lesson. His frail booth was but poor protection from the beating sun, and so:

> The Lord God prepared a gourd, and made it to come up over Jonah, that it might be a shadow over his head, to deliver him from his grief. So Jonah was exceeding glad of the gourd (Jonah 4:6).

In studying the Book of Jonah we find that he was a man of opposite moods. First he was exceedingly angry because his pride had been injured. Now he is exceedingly "glad" over a frail plant which grew up overnight.

However, God did not prepare the gourd primarily to make Jonah glad, but rather to teach him a lesson, to rebuke his selfishness, for no sooner had Jonah settled down comfortably beneath the gourd than:

> God prepared a worm when the morning rose the next day, and it smote the gourd that it withered.
>
> And it came to pass, when the sun did arise, that God prepared a vehement (sultry hot) east wind; and the sun beat upon the head of Jonah, that he fainted, and wished in himself to die, and said, It is better for me to die than to live (Jonah 4:7, 8).

One moment this fickle prophet is "exceeding glad." The next moment he wants to die. Oh, the patience and the longsuffering of God as seen in this record. How He bears with poor Jonah, His servant. How gracious the Lord had been with him. He had tried to run away from God, he had reluctantly preached to Nineveh; he rejoiced in their destruction; he took issue with God; he accused God of not keeping His Word; he had failed and blundered at every turn. He himself deserved nothing but judgment and damnation, but God in infinite mercy still cared for him. All this was to prepare Jonah for the lesson he needed so much to learn. Listen to God's words to Jonah:

Then said the Lord, Thou hast had pity on the gourd, for the which thou hast not laboured, neither madest it grow; which came up in a night, and perished in a night:

And should not I spare Nineveh, that great city, wherein are more than sixscore thousand persons that cannot discern between their right hand and their left hand; and also much cattle? (Jonah 4:10, 11)

Little needs to be added to this brief account with which the Book of Jonah ends. The lesson is so evident on the surface that no one can miss it. God seems to say, "Listen, Jonah, you have pity for the gourd because you were deprived of its shade. Why then be angry when I have pity on a great city of a million people destined for eternity, and am willing to save them from destruction?"

First Things First

"Remember, therefore, Jonah, how patiently I have borne with you, in your disobedience, your rebellion, your murmuring, and your bigoted selfishness. Suppose I should deal with you in justice. You would be consigned to hell today, but in my mercy and grace and longsuffering, in spite of all your unworthiness and rebellion, I have made you an object of my love and salvation and care; and do you now object to my doing the same for others? Shame on you, Jonah; double shame on you for your attitude. How can you, who are just as unworthy as these heathen, be so indifferent? You are an even greater sinner than they for you know the Lord and His will and His Word, and you are acting worse than these poor heathen who have never had the chance that you obtained of the Lord."

Make It Personal

To all of this, I am sure, every one of us will subscribe. Give poor Jonah his due, rip him apart, for he deserves it. But listen! All the time that I have been talking about Jonah, I have been talking about YOU. We are all too content to apply all this to someone else, but how about YOU, and ME! If you

are a Christian, God has called you to tell the world about the
Death and the Resurrection of His Son, Jesus Christ, of whom
Jonah was a type. It was to you that He said:

Go ye into all the world, and preach the gospel to every
creature (Mark 16:15).

Have WE obeyed that command? Until we have, we had
better "lay off" poor old Jonah, and turn the searchlight
upon ourselves. We say that we have been saved, we rejoice
in our salvation, and yet how little we have been concerned
about others who have never heard. Too often it is true of
many of us, that we like Jonah are occupied with material
comforts and pleasures, and have no vision of a lost and
dying world. How much are we doing to win others? How
much do we pray for the lost, even in our own family? How
much time do we spend in speaking to others about the
Lord Jesus Christ? How much do we give, that the Gospel
may go forth to all the world? Stop, for a moment, my friend,
and take an inventory of your own accomplishments. Your
chief concern has been your home, your success, your temporal
security, the search for pleasure, while millions and millions
are going to hell because you have been building booths on the
east side of the city for your own ease and comfort.

There is but little time left. The forty days of grace will
soon be past. Judgment, we believe, is impending. The
rumbling of the thunders of the Tribulation are intensifying,
and the storm clouds of judgment are gathering upon the
horizon. We must hasten, for the forty days of probation
of this dispensation are almost up. Ask yourself, How much
am I doing to make this message known, by personal testimony,
prayer, distribution of the Gospel, and every other available
means which the Lord has placed at my disposal?

In closing, a personal word to the sinner. Jonah, of course,
is a picture of God's wonderful, infinite grace for a poor,
blundering prophet. Nineveh also deserved judgment, but
because they believed God and repented of their sin, God in

mercy and pity spared them. You too are under condemnation, and soon the day of grace will end for you. Your "forty days" will soon come to an end. It may be even today. Oh, turn to Him now, and remember that:

> God sent not his Son into the world to condemn the world; but that the world through him might be saved.
>
> He that believeth on him is not condemned: but he that believeth not is condemned already, because he hath not believed in the name of the only begotten Son of God.
>
> And this is the condemnation, that light is come into the world, and men loved darkness rather than light, because their deeds were evil (John 3:17-19).

Why not trust Him now and be saved?

Then Christian brother, sister, will you rouse to the urgency of the task? Unless we do, like the sailors, the world will be saying to us:

> What meanest thou, O sleeper? arise, call upon thy God, if so be that God will think upon us, that we perish not (Jonah 1:6).

And thus the Book of Jonah ends as abruptly as it began. We know practically nothing about Jonah's early life, and the Bible is silent concerning his last years. What happened to Jonah? Did he learn his lesson? How long after did he live? To all these questions the Bible gives no answer, for the application is to us. We are not to be concerned with Jonah, but to apply it to our own hearts, and ask ourselves the question, Have we learned OUR lesson? Will we repent of our selfishness and indifference? How much time is left for us, and what will we do with it? God grant that we may benefit by the record of Jonah.

> Wherefore he saith, Awake thou that sleepest, and arise from the dead, and Christ shall give thee light.
>
> See then that ye walk circumspectly, not as fools, but as wise, Redeeming the time, because the days are evil.
>
> Wherefore be ye not unwise, but understanding what the will of the Lord is (Eph. 5:14-17).